Le

Pain

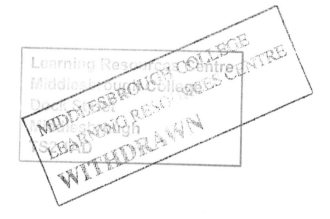

**Key Themes in Health and Social Care series**

Alan Cribb and Sharon Gewirtz, *Professionalism*
Nick Fox, *The Body*
Janet Hargreaves and Louise Page, *Reflective Practice*

# Pain
## A Sociological Introduction

ELAINE DENNY

polity

First published in 2018 by Polity Press

Polity Press
65 Bridge Street
Cambridge CB2 1UR, UK

Polity Press
101 Station Landing
Suite 300
Medford, MA 02155
USA

ISBN-13: 978-0-7456-5554-3
ISBN-13: 978-0-7456-5555-0(pb)

A catalogue record for this book is available from the British Library.

Library of Congress Cataloging-in-Publication Data

Names: Denny, Elaine, author.
Title: Pain : a sociological introduction / Elaine Denny.
Description: Medford, MA : Polity Press, [2017] | Includes bibliographical references and index.
Identifiers: LCCN 2017021111 (print) | LCCN 2017022759 (ebook) | ISBN 9781509527212 (Mobi) | ISBN 9781509527229 (Epub) | ISBN 9780745655543 (hardback) | ISBN 9780745655550 (pbk.)
Subjects: LCSH: Pain. | Pain--Social aspects.
Classification: LCC BF515 (ebook) | LCC BF515 .D466 2017 (print) | DDC 306.4/61--dc23
LC record available at https://lccn.loc.gov/2017021111

Typeset in 10.25 on 13 pt Scala
by Servis Filmsetting Ltd, Stockport, Cheshire
Printed and bound in Great Britain by Clays Ltd, St. Ives PLC

For further information on Polity, visit our website: www.politybooks.com

# Contents

# Introduction

Pain in one form or another is probably the most common symptom presented to healthcare professionals and has long been a subject of biomedical and psychological interest. More recently, biopsychosocial theories of pain have also emerged. The work of Melzack and Wall (1965, 1968) in describing and refining 'gate-control theory' has been very influential in extending the study of pain beyond a measurable concept to one which is highly individual in the way it is experienced. However, this work has been set within a naturalistic framework, and only much more recently has a sociological analysis of pain been attempted. While students in the natural and social science disciplines have access to discrete bodies of knowledge, students in the health professions, and indeed people searching for explanations for their own pain, tend to make use of an eclectic mix of theoretical and practical work. This can, however, lead to confusion over seemingly disputed territory and conflicting arguments and conclusions. Making sense of the competing arguments may be a difficult task for people not versed in appraising different forms of evidence. With that in mind, this volume seeks to be accessible without being simplistic.

To that end, I will begin by clarifying how certain terms will be used in the book. 'Clinicians' or 'health professionals' are used as generic terms for physiotherapists, nurses, doctors, etc., working in clinical practice. The phrases 'long-term condition or illness' or 'chronic disease or illness' reflect how the terminology has changed as ideas about those living with these states of health have changed. I tend to employ the terms used in the studies I cite, but in other places adopt the common distinction between 'disease' and 'illness': the former understood as a medically diagnosed condition, the latter as the experience of living with health problems. However, it must be acknowledged that there is no clear boundary between 'normal' and 'pathological', and it is this that frequently results in tensions in health and healthcare.

You will also come across concepts that are problematised in some parts of the book but used uncritically in others, such as that of diagnosis. Similarly, in some places it may seem that binary oppositions such as that between acute and chronic pain are not being challenged as false divisions. These concepts and distinctions are so universal and hegemonic that the English language does not always offer alternative terms that would allow us to recognise the contested nature of the dominant discourse that surrounds them. Where relevant, I have highlighted the contested nature of these concepts, but elsewhere, in order to avoid repetition, I have left them unchallenged.

Finally, the word 'experience' is used frequently throughout the book, and its meaning may appear to be somewhat taken for granted. Unless interpreted differently in relation to the studies cited, I adopt the definition given by Kleinman and Seeman, who argue that 'experience' is not 'a deep and individual subjectivity', but rather represents 'the intersubjective, felt flow of events, bodily processes, and life trajectory which always takes place within a social context' (2000: 234). Here the link between the personal, the cultural and the social is acknowledged: experience does not take place in a vacuum, but is mediated by cultural and social structures, which will be utilised to explore individual narratives.

Much of the medical research on pain has been conducted using quantitative methods, and although this provides information on large numbers of people, it tends to lack context. Sociological research in the area has mainly utilised qualitative approaches. This does not produce results that can be generalised to the wider population, but it does give us insight and understanding in relation to the world of those living with pain, the meaning it has in their life, and how they make sense of it. It can also seem that the results of such research are usually negative, but, as C. S. Lewis states, 'Pain hurts. That's what the word means' (1940: 105). It may be that those who are in the most extreme forms of pain, or those whose pain is not managed well, are more likely to take part in research that gives them a voice.

If you suffer from pain, particularly long-term pain, you may find that parts of this book, or the individual stories it presents, resonate with your own experience, or help you to understand or make sense of your life. Unfortunately, though, you will not find a new treatment to try, or anything that will ease your pain. The book is an exploration and examination of various facets of pain from a sociological perspective. There are many authors and researchers on pain whom I have not cited, and one criticism of the study may be that I have neglected a classic text or respected authority. My focus here is on an exploration of pain that attempts to be illuminative, rather than exhaustive, in its use of the literature.

My own interest in exploring pain began in the late 1980s when I was researching women's experience of in vitro fertilisation (IVF). I interviewed a woman and her husband who had – at great expense, both financial and personal – gone through three cycles of IVF, all of which had been unsuccessful. It was then discovered that the woman suffered from endometriosis, which meant that the IVF could never have worked for her. Her husband told me that his wife had always experienced very painful menstruation, which they had repeatedly informed health professionals about, and which should have led to a faster diagnosis and treatment prior to IVF. However, his wife's pain was never taken seriously; she was fobbed off and told that the pain was psychological and caused by her inability to conceive. This is a story I have heard many times since, as will become apparent later in the book. At the time I was left wondering how a symptom such as severe pain could be totally ignored and trivialised in the management of a patient, particularly when treatment is proving unsuccessful. It was some years later that I had the opportunity to explore these issues further, when I started research with other women who had been diagnosed with endometriosis. I discovered that the way pain is experienced and managed is highly complex and multi-layered, with assumptions and value judgements made by those experiencing pain, by those treating them, and by their significant others.

More recently I have been involved in teaching a module on the sociology and psychology of pain to health professionals studying for an MSc in pain management. The assessment involved students taking an aspect of practice relating to pain (anything from a case study to an area of health policy) and analysing it using the psychological and sociological concepts introduced in the module. Students could quite easily apply psychology to their chosen topic, but frequently had problems in seeing the relevance of sociology to what they perceived as the very personal nature of experiencing pain. However, when they discussed their assessment topics with other students and staff it usually became apparent that there were situations where a sociological analysis was a useful tool in the understanding of pain. This book is the culmination of those discussions with students and of my research, both empirical and theoretical, in relation to pain over the past fifteen years.

Bendelow (2000) argues that the most salient role for a sociology of pain is to deconstruct the rigid objectivity of the biomedical model, and to restore pain to those who actually experience it. This is what I hope to achieve by using a range of sociological concepts and empirical studies to explore the subject. Nearly 50 million Americans report suffering significant or severe chronic pain, and those with the worst levels of pain – around 40 million – have poorer health status, use more health services, and suffer more disability than those with less severe pain (Nahin, 2015). In Europe approximately 20 per cent of the adult population has chronic pain and, besides the physical and emotional cost to the individual and their family, managing it is estimated to cost more than €200 million (Van Hecke et al., 2013). A systematic review of the incidence of chronic pain in the UK suggests that between one third and one half of the adult population are affected by it, with between 10.4 per cent and 14.3 per cent reporting pain that is moderately or severely limiting (Fayaz et al., 2016).

Away from the wealthier countries of the West, chronic pain is becoming a greater health problem, as lower rates of infectious disease mean more people live into old age. Chronic pain is associated with female gender, older age (although the incidence of lower-back pain decreases with age), ethnicity and lower socio-economic status (Bridges, 2012). Fewer than 20 per cent of chronic pain sufferers attend a specialist pain clinic (Van Hecke et al., 2013). Physically, emotionally and economically, long-term pain is one of the most pressing public health issues of the twenty-first century, and is likely to become more so with greater longevity, as people spend more years of life with some degree of incapacity.

Chapter 1 sets the scene by providing an overview of pain in its historical context, some of which still has relevance today. Pain has been viewed over the centuries as a punishment from God and as evidence of sin, particularly the sin of carnal knowledge, through to Enlightenment theories, the hegemony of the scientific method, and recent explanatory models such as the neuromatrix.

In Chapter 2 we move towards a sociological paradigm by considering the work of some of the founding thinkers in sociology, as well as more recent developments in the study of pain that have moved away from the theoretical positions of the past towards more relational approaches.

Chapter 3 is concerned with the experience of pain. It starts by considering some of the ways in which sociologists have conceptualised pain, for example as biographical disruption. Here we review some of the sociological work that has captured the lives of people living with pain, how it affects their families, and the stories they tell to make sense of their experience and to inform others of its impact.

Chapter 4 moves away from the individual to think about care and carers. It looks at the provision of services, both public and private, and the pluralistic nature of provision. Here we also consider the perspective of those who live with, and perhaps care for, a person in pain.

Since the way in which pain is experienced and interpreted is not universal, Chapter 5 explores the structures of diversity and the ways in which they influence the experience of pain. The impact of gender, age and ethnicity on the experience of pain will be the focus of this chapter. However, the importance of not essentialising any one social categorisation, and not treating people as powerless agents in relation to their culture or gender, will also be acknowledged.

Chapter 6 will consider those whose pain is marginalised, and the way they describe their own experience and make sense of it in the context of their lives. Many people never receive an explanation for their pain. The consequences of being labelled as having 'unexplained pain' and the way that people respond to it – for example by striving to be believed and viewed as credible patients – will be explored using recent qualitative studies on the experience of painful conditions.

In Chapter 7 we move away from discussing the physical pain that is the focus of most of the chapters. For some individuals, and some health professionals, the pain they experience or encounter is emotional, and recently attention has been drawn to suffering as a painful part of life. While avoiding a dualistic approach to pain as being either physical or emotional, this chapter will look at some of the recent research on emotional pain and suffering. It will also reflect on the increasing medicalisation of that suffering.

Chapter 8 will turn from the person in pain to consider the perspective of the health professionals who treat them. It will examine how health professionals interpret and respond to pain, contrasting this with the patients' perspectives discussed

in previous chapters. How the meaning of pain and its interpretation may differ between patients and their doctors will
be shown to influence the quality of communication during
health consultations, and may also affect treatment.

Finally, in the Conclusion, I bring together the topics of the
previous chapters and draw some conclusions about viewing
pain through a sociological lens.

# CHAPTER ONE

# Historical Perspectives on Pain

Before examining its place in the modern world it is worth taking a brief look at pain in a historical context, because, as Abrams (1982) argues, serious questions about the contemporary world cannot adequately be answered without reference to history. The purpose of this chapter is not to provide a detailed analysis of pain in different historical periods, but to demonstrate the changing nature of perceptions and interpretations of pain, and how these are bound up with social context and with dominant ideas that are culturally and historically specific. As such, the examples discussed in what follows are illustrative rather than representative. The chapter is also unashamedly Eurocentric, since attempting to provide a global history of pain would be an impossible task in a volume such as this. Some comparative analysis will, however, feature in Chapter 5.

Healing work was the forerunner of the health-work systems that we know today, and was much more informal in nature. It was carried out by many different people – e.g. bone setters or herbalists – who competed with doctors for custom. Most healing work was domestic in nature, performed by women, and usually unpaid. While acknowledging that these different healers would have been involved in the relief of pain throughout history, the main occupational group considered in this book will be the medical profession. This is because its development and hegemony in defining and legitimising illness was a continuation of the professionalising project of the period since the Enlightenment. Doctors were historically few in number – there were fewer than 100 physicians outside

London before the eighteenth century – and were available to only a small proportion of the population, but their importance grew as they increasingly gained jurisdiction over health work, and excluded or incorporated other types of healer. However, as we will go on to discuss, this did not occur because doctors were more successful than other healers at curing patients, since their domination occurred before many effective therapies were available.

## Issues in the study of history

First, we need to highlight some of the problems inherent in taking a historical stance towards an issue. We should always bear in mind who wrote accounts that have been preserved, with what purpose, and how representative of society they were. Rafferty, for example, notes 'a bias towards the preservation of evidence by those classes whose culture is mediated through the written rather than spoken word' (1995: 52). Since the majority of the population was illiterate before the introduction of mass education in the 1870s, those classes were restricted mainly to the rich and the clergy, who had access to education.

Second, care should be taken to avoid the problem of present-centredness. That is, in seeking to study history we are necessarily taking as our starting point the knowledge and values of the present, which may not be relevant to the past. The period and context of historical documents need to be considered. Judgements based on present-day values may not elicit reliable meanings in relation to the standpoints of previous generations. Here, this will mean questioning contemporary notions of 'pain', 'suffering', 'mind', 'body' and 'spirit' when considering the historical uses of such terms.

A quick look through the indexes of recent books on the history of medicine – including those by Roy Porter, the eminent former Professor of the Social History of Medicine at the Wellcome Institute – reveals a dearth of entries for pain. Porter himself, in one of his few chapters on pain (written with his wife Dorothy), offers some insight into why this might be. Although some people did record their ailments, what was written down is selective and misleading, as those with the most profound symptoms had neither the strength nor the desire to record them. Some chronic pains are the exception here, for example gout, of which there are many descriptions (Porter and Porter, 1988).

## Concepts of pain in antiquity

Although there is a lack of historical publications on pain, a classic text on the history of pain was published in 1993 in Paris, a few months before the death of the author from cancer, aged forty-three. In it Roselyne Rey (1995) traces the cultural perception of pain from antiquity to the twentieth century, although her focus is mainly on physical pain. Her treatise begins with the Hippocratic tradition of ancient Greece, which continued to be the bedrock of scientific medical education until the middle of the nineteenth century. Here pain is seen not as an isolated symptom, but as part of an overall assessment of how the patient looks, of their behaviour compared to how they generally behave, and of their bodily fluids, such as urine and sweat. This system of medicine placed great importance on prognosis, and the doctor's success was judged on how well he predicted the course of disease. Pain was viewed as a vital clue in this endeavour, as well as being an indicator of the success or failure of treatment when it subsided or intensified, but it was given no other significance. Treatments for pain included the application of heat or cold, cauterisation of the painful part, and the use of narcotic herbs. Hippocratic ideas were widely disseminated throughout Asia Minor and to the rest of the known world. The work of Galen in the second century CE placed great importance on pain, both as a symptom and a mechanism. He introduced different classifications of pain that are still in use in modified form, for example 'pulsific' (throbbing) and 'tensive' (stretching) (Rey, 1995).

Rey argues that despite developing a knowledge base about the body, and classifying different forms of pain, ancient medicine did not reach any conclusions about its usefulness. This she puts down to the fact that it was based in the rival philosophical traditions of Epicureanism and Stoicism, neither of which believed that there was any value in the experience of pain. Of the two traditions, Stoicism is the most useful in tracing perceptions of pain through the ages, since its ideas on pain persisted for many centuries. For the Stoics the production of knowledge emerged from reason and a communing with nature. A belief in self-control and virtue was seen as necessary for human fulfilment. Their attitude to pain was to endure it and not become preoccupied with it. We still hear people use the term 'stoical' to describe someone who puts up with pain or hardship without complaint.

## Pain and Christian teaching

During the Middle Ages Stoicism became linked with Christian ideas in the Western world, and the Galenic tradition influenced both the West and the Arab world. Within Europe the Christian preoccupation with Christ's suffering may have heralded a more individualistic approach to pain, which certainly flourished during the Renaissance. Pain reminded Christians to empathise with Christ on the Cross (Newton, 2011).

In Britain, Christian teaching rooted in the notion of Divine Providence had a major influence on perceptions of pain and its meaning right up to the nineteenth century. Put simply, the idea was that God in his omniscience controls all that occurs in the universe, good and bad (McCann, 2012), and that the existence of evil or suffering can thus be explained by its having a higher purpose. These ideas survived despite the changing attitudes of the Enlightenment and the growth of scientific explanation. They are examined by the historian Hannah Newton in her work on the pain experienced by children, who are rarely the focus of historiography on patienthood, despite the high incidence of child mortality up to the end of the nineteenth century. She points to the paradox within Christian beliefs about the meaning of sickness: 'On the one hand, sickness was often painful, frightening, and a source of spiritual guilt and grief, but on the other hand, it could be a time of spiritual and emotional fulfilment, and even occasionally joy' (Newton, 2011: 154). If God brought pain as punishment for sin, then the sick also experienced guilt as they had brought it upon themselves. It was necessary for the sufferer to dwell upon these sins so that once they repented the sickness would be taken away. Examples of sins that children admitted to were not going to bed when their mother told them to, gluttony, and playing on the Sabbath. Children's sickness could also be seen as resulting from the sins of their parents. The more positive effect of Divine Providence would be the emotional and spiritual comfort to be gained from the knowledge that something good would come from suffering. While the body may be hurting, its suffering is benefiting the soul by purging sin and leading to salvation in the afterlife. So pain could be suffered willingly or with resignation.

Newton's examples come from devout, wealthy or middle-class Puritan families and may not be representative of the population, even though religiosity was widespread during the period covered (1580–1720) (Newton, 2011). Rey argues that it was the birth of the notion of the individual during the Renaissance that allowed a shift in the understanding of pain: no longer was it seen as part of a wider purpose but as something residing within the individual. It is this latter view which has been perpetuated through the development of science and the biomedical model, to which we now turn.

## The Enlightenment

The Enlightenment period heralded a move away from the dominance of the Church in explaining events and phenomena, and a move towards the era of rationality and science (Rey,

1995). The development of observation and secularisation became dominant features that changed the conceptualisation of pain. Reason determined the development of ideas, observation, and experimentation on the sick, and the dissection of dead bodies added to anatomical and medical knowledge at an impressive rate. Yet, as Porter (1997) informs us, Enlightenment thinking in medicine was not monolithic, and there were many rival camps throughout Europe and America. He also points out that scientific findings were rarely accompanied by clinical improvements, which may account for the continued influence of religion noted by Newton.

Here we can offer only a very superficial description of the Enlightenment and the way it influenced thinking, but for our purposes in documenting shifts in the perception and interpretation of pain, the important point is that the era brought about a change in the way the body was viewed: from being seen as an instrument of the soul to a more mechanistic view of it as a machine operating according to natural laws. Proponents of this new thinking such as René Descartes and Isaac Newton argued that these laws were pre-existing and that discovering them would lead to a complete understanding and predictability of man [sic] and the universe. An example of this is Cartesian dualism, which held that mind and body are distinct and each is complete; that is, each can be understood without reference to the other (Hawthorne, 2007). It is often oversimplified as a mind–body split. Cartesian dualism has been widely critiqued within the sociology of pain, notably by Gillian Bendelow, and discussion of this issue will be found in several of the following chapters. Porter, however, plays down the influence of Descartes, at least in Britain, and argues that Locke's empiricism, which emphasised the gaining of knowledge through experience, was more influential in advancing scientific investigation (Porter, 2000). Scientific explanations of pain did not, however, replace earlier thinking overnight; they co-existed with religious interpretations into the twentieth century, and indeed to some extent still do.

During the Enlightenment era treatments for pain moved away from purges and confessions of sin. While alcohol was the most common substance used for pain relief, the eighteenth century became 'the golden age of medically prescribed opiates', even though they had their own drawbacks in terms of being addictive and causing intestinal problems (Porter and Porter, 1988: 102). Opium was ubiquitous, mainly in the form of tinctures such as laudanum, and fairly freely available despite the fact that some of its uses were dubious and even criminal. It was taken to relieve menstrual cramps, given to babies to make them sleep, and used for many other reasons. It is often mentioned in nineteenth-century literature; for example, Mary Shelley's Dr Frankenstein takes it to help him sleep, and the moonstone in Wilkie Collins' novel of the same name is stolen by Franklin Blake after he is secretly given laudanum.

Debates were had over whether pain should be treated with 'the same' or 'the opposite' (similar to homeopathy) (Rey, 1995: 128). For example, the hot pain of inflammation was treated by the application of the cold qualities of narcotics, while for the pain of gangrene more pain was inflicted by the procedure of amputation, which was necessary for healing. Despite these divergent views on treatments, there was a consensus in Enlightenment thinking that the experience of pain was unacceptable and must be eliminated. Within the dominant culture of reason it seemed to serve no purpose, and was something that the medical profession had to confront, even if this involved inflicting more pain (Rey, 1995).

## Disappearance of the sick-man

This historical shift in the meaning of pain has been described by Jewson as 'the disappearance of the sick-man [sic]' (1976: 225). He argues that between 1770 and 1870 (although these are indicative rather than exact dates) there were three modes of production of medical knowledge, each associated with a particular cosmology (or way of knowing) that determined the knowledge that was produced. At the start of the period Bedside Medicine focused on the total body complex – physical, emotional and spiritual – with the mind and body being viewed as part of the same system of pathology. Medical practitioners speculated on the interpretation of symptoms and provided individualised therapies. Hospital Medicine developed as a result of the medical upheaval in France following the French Revolution, which led to the growth of institutionalised medicine. Disease became objectified, facilitated by having many patients in one place who could be observed and examined, by developments in pathology with a focus on diseased organs rather than the whole person, and by the development of statistical analysis. The third mode of medical cosmology, Laboratory Medicine, developed in German universities from the 1840s and was concerned with diagnoses made from the study of the physiological processes within cells. So this trajectory has an orientation from 'person to object orientated cosmologies' (Jewson, 1976: 231) – a reductionist approach that has seen the focus shift from the whole person, through diseased organs, to abnormalities within cells as holding the key to diagnosis. It also saw a change in power relationships as the esoteric scientific knowledge that was the exclusive preserve of the medical profession achieved greater status than the experiential knowledge of the patient.

## Foucault and the birth of the clinic

The French philosopher Michel Foucault (1973) also associated the move to locate illness within the body with the period around the French Revolution and the growth of pathological anatomy. In *The Birth of the Clinic*, Foucault uses the concept of 'the gaze' (or *le regard* in the original French) to describe a way of seeing the body which is constructed by a discourse of disease becoming visible to the clinician (see Chapter 2 for a discussion on 'discourse'). As a form of knowledge this was facilitated by 'a reorganisation of the hospital field, a new

definition of the status of the patient in society, and the establishment of a certain relationship between public assistance
and medical experience, between help and knowledge' (1973:
196).

The years following the French Revolution saw an increase
in the numbers of poor people receiving medical treatment free
within the large teaching hospitals (the clinics of the book's
title) run by municipal administrations. This allowed doctors
to observe large numbers of people, collect information about
them, and group this according to pathological similarities. It
also allowed them to experiment on a class of patients who
did not possess the power to refuse. Perhaps most impor-
tantly, symptoms apparent before death could be aligned with
pathological changes in organs that could be observed in post-
mortem examinations. The clinical gaze thus located disease
within the body, but this was only possible thanks to the symbi-
otic relationship between body, disease and a specific medical
discourse that emerged in post-revolutionary France. Medical
discourse at any time is not the result of a gradual unfolding of
knowledge but a shift in the way that knowledge is constructed.
As Armstrong argued: 'A body analysed for humours contains
humours; a body analysed for organs and tissues is constituted
by organs and tissues; a body analysed for psychosocial functioning is a psychosocial object' (1994: 25).

The institution of the major teaching hospital as the location
of large numbers of patients and thus the site of the medical
gaze quickly spread to other parts of Europe and subsequently
to other parts of the world. As will become apparent in later
chapters, the medical discourse that emerged from this institution still influences the practice of medicine today.

## The pain of surgery

It was during the nineteenth century that the greatest advances
in understanding pain and developing treatments were made.
Driven by scientific thinking, experimentation was under

way in Britain, Europe and America on ways of reducing pain, particularly during surgery. Before this time surgery was only undertaken in dire emergencies when there was no other option, as in the case of gangrene, or for external procedures such as lancing boils. Much of the surgery took place on the battlefields of war-obsessed Europe, providing plenty of practice for surgeons to hone their skills. Surgery became a theatrical performance (hence the name 'theatre' for where it is undertaken), with top surgeons attracting not only medical students to watch an amputation but also the public at large. Porter (1997) explains that skill and speed were the only answer to limiting the excruciating pain, citing James Syme, who could reputedly amputate a leg in ninety seconds. During the early nineteenth century more invasive procedures – e.g. removal of ovarian cysts, repair of cleft palate, hysterectomy – were carried out with only opium or alcohol as pain relief, but mortality was high from infection or shock.

To get some idea of the horror of surgery before the introduction of anaesthetics we can turn to the diaries of Fanny Burney, in which she gives a graphic account of having a mastectomy in 1811. Because of the terror which surgery held for the patient, she was not told of the timing of the operation until two hours before it took place. There is no record in her diaries of her being given anything other than wine and cordial for the pain before the mastectomy was performed. In a letter to her sister Esther she wrote:

> When the dreadful steel was plunged into the breast – cutting through veins – arteries – flesh – nerves – I needed no injunctions not to restrain my cries. I began a scream that lasted unintermittingly during the whole time of the incision – and I almost marvel that it rings not in my Ears still! so excruciating was the agony (Hemlow, 1975: 612).

Fanny continues to describe how each time that she thought the operation was over 'the terrible cutting was renewed' (Hemlow, 1975: 612). Lasting 3 hours, 45 minutes, this was not the rapid surgery of amputation, and according to the surgeon's pupil who wrote an account of the operation, it 'was very painful and endured with much courage' (Hemlow, 1975: 616, my translation). For months Fanny could not speak about the operation without reliving it and being sick. She did, however, survive a further thirty-eight years, dying at the age of ninety-six. It was the discovery of anaesthetic agents, such as ether and chloroform (both of which could give rise to serious complications), that facilitated the development of more effective surgical techniques and allowed surgeons to take the time to control bleeding. Harold Ellis, Emeritus Professor of Surgery at Guy's Hospital, London, writes:

> If you should ask me to name the most important date in the whole history of surgery, I would reply, without a moment's hesitation, Friday October 16th 1846. The operation was a simple, almost trivial procedure, the removal of a small benign lump in the neck, but it marked the watershed between the past agonies of surgery and the modern era, where our patients enjoy the blissful oblivion of anaesthesia. (Ellis, 2010: 302)

The use of anaesthetic agents was not universally welcomed, however, a key example being their use during labour. Queen Victoria had been given chloroform during the birth of her eighth child, following which there were many protests. From a religious standpoint it was argued that it was ordained by God that women should bring forth children in pain. The objection from doctors was that the risk of contractions being stopped by the administration of chloroform could not justify its use during a normal labour. However, for both surgery and childbirth chloroform continued to be given to reduce pain until the development of more reliable analgesia and anaesthetics.

## The hysterical woman

It is no accident that the removal of the uterus is called not a 'uterectomy', as many women think it should be, but a hysterectomy, and that hysteria has long been used as a term for female madness. Hippocrates was the first to use the word 'hysteria' to describe compulsive movements of the body caused by abnormal movements of the uterus. These in turn were thought to be caused by stagnant humours which had not been expelled due to inadequate sexual activity, sex being one way that excess humours left the body (Tasca et al., 2012). Sex and childbirth were believed to keep the uterus healthy by cleansing the body. Hippocrates argued further that in virgins, widows and single or infertile women this was compounded by the uterus wandering round the body causing such symptoms as anxiety, a sense of suffocation, tremors, convulsions and paralysis (Tasca et al., 2012). This view of hysteria persisted through the Middle Ages and the Renaissance, and in 1651 William Harvey wrote that delirium, melancholy and paroxysms of frenzy were caused by unnatural states of the uterus (Pollak, 2013). It was the physician Thomas Sydenham who disassociated hysteria and the uterus, and noted that the former was frequently seen as a disease of the nervous system. The link persisted, however, and the term 'uterine neurosis' was used to describe it (Da Mota Gomes and Engelhardt, 2014). In the nineteenth century the French neurologist Jean-Martin Charcot described hysteria as a hereditary condition triggered by some traumatic life event. In spite of the fact that many of his case studies were women, Freud (who studied under Charcot) believed that hysteria was a condition affecting both men and women, and even described it in himself (Da Mota Gomes and Engelhardt, 2014). Freud characterised hysteria as being the result of a traumatic sexual event in childhood, which remain repressed until something, usually an adult sexual relationship, triggered the latent hysteria, producing the physical symptoms with which many of his patients presented. He advocated the use of psychoanalysis to elicit the initial sexual abuse and cause the symptoms to improve.

During the latter quarter of the nineteenth century and into the twentieth many women were treated for hysteria by removal of their ovaries and/or uterus. An American surgeon,

Robert Batty, developed 'normal' ovariotomy, in which normal ovaries were removed in women diagnosed as hysterical or neurotic (Porter, 1997). Pollak states: 'It seems unthinkable now that gynaecological "cures" for hysteria were regularly practiced before they fell out of clinical favour. The weight and influence of centuries of misogynistic theorising by an all-male medical establishment should not be underestimated' (2013: 1). Although many of these ideas and treatments may be outdated, women may still find that they are labelled neurotic or hysterical within the health system. This will be explored further in Chapters 5 and 6.

## The early twentieth century

Early twentieth-century research on nerves and synaptic transmission, and pharmaceutical developments in synthetic analgesics such as aspirin, were a continuation of the scientific discoveries of the nineteenth century and firmly locate pain within a biomedical model. This research was the precursor to the dominant theories that subsequently emerged over the following half century, such as gate-control theory, which will be discussed in the next section. Existing knowledge on pain was also incorporated into newly emerging medical fields such as endocrinology, which demonstrated the somatic changes that could occur with the experience of pain. This twentieth-century research also marked a shift away from the idea of pain as serving no purpose, viewing it in a positive light as having an evolutionary rationale (Rey, 1995). Since the lack of a pain response would leave individuals vulnerable to threats from without, pain becomes interpreted as a warning system that produces a response, such as pulling a hand away from a hot kettle. It also warns of things going wrong within the body that cannot be seen externally.

Theories of pain formulated during this period, such as the specificity theory and the pattern theory, had their supporters, but they could not be demonstrated to work empirically, and in any case by this time purely mechanistic models were giving way to the idea that pain had a psychosocial as well as biomedical basis (Gatchel and Maddrey, 2004). The specificity theory, for example, assumed a linear pathway from the skin to the brain in which it was purely the severity of injury that was reflected in the level of pain.

The mid-twentieth century also saw the emergence of pain as an object for medical treatment in itself, as distinct from treating the cause. This shift in emphasis required that pain be 'endowed with unique characteristics that would give it a new status' (Baszanger, 1998: 2). Specifically this involved separating clinical pain from laboratory pain, and acute pain from chronic pain. This led to the creation of pain as a clinical specialism, and pain clinics as the location for managing it, as will be explored in Chapter 4.

## The gate-control theory of pain

Baszanger (1998) argues that the development of the gate-control theory was an essential tool in opening up the study of pain on three fronts: research, medicine and psychology. This theory, introduced by Ronald Melzack and Patrick Wall in 1965, was the first to consider the interaction of physiological and psychosocial variables in the production of pain (Melzack and Wall, 1968). Although it was initially challenged as incomplete, various reformulations of the original model have meant that it has continued to be the most widely used theory of pain (Gatchel, 2013). The physiological basis of the theory is that pain receptors at the site of the pain (skin, muscles, organs) transmit information about the damage to a series of metaphorical 'gates' in the spinal column, which in turn link to other nerves taking the message up to the brain. At the same time, the other sensations we experience (fear, shock, anxiety) result in information being passed in the opposite direction, from the brain to the gate. The pain that is experienced is dependent on the physiological factors that open the gate, but also on the downward pathway, which also influences the position of the gate. So factors such as previous experience, expectations and cultural norms will all affect how much pain is felt in a given situation. This work led to the development of the McGill Pain Questionnaire as a pain assessment tool (Crawford, 2009), which will be critiqued in Chapter 4.

More recently Melzack (2001) has formulated the 'neuro-matrix' theory of pain, which moves on from the gate-control theory and seeks to explain chronic pain experiences in which there may be no discernible injury or pathology. In particular, Melzack wanted to account for the mechanisms of phantom-limb pain, and to that end proposed a neuromatrix, or network, of at least three neural circuits involved in the production of pain intensity, which is genetically determined. However, since psychological and social influences may also impact on this to produce an individual's experience of pain, in recent years additional neural circuits have been added, implying that many areas of the brain are involved in the production of pain.

## Summary

In this brief historical overview we have seen how ideas about the causes and meaning of pain are not fixed and static, but change over time – from it being seen as God-given and a punishment for sin, to Enlightenment views of it as serving no rational purpose, to current thinking which interprets pain as a warning or indication of some disease or bodily malfunction. The patient in pain has also been interpreted in different ways over time, and the relative power of patient and doctor has shifted as medicine has developed, via the medical gaze, what some would describe as an esoteric knowledge not accessible to patients. However, physiological accounts of pain production have continued to dominate, although there is increasing acknowledgement of other factors, which has led to the development of the biopsychosocial model to be discussed in Chapter 7. As stated at the start of this chapter, the purpose of taking a historical overview is to locate the following chapters within a continuum. Doing so also demonstrates that the way we think about pain, make sense of it and understand it changes over time, not just because of increasing knowledge, but due to changes in the way we view the world and how those changes determine the construction of knowledge. The mid-twentieth-century shift from viewing pain as a symptom to be treated by addressing the cause to seeing it as a focus of medical attention in its own right has had a major impact on the provision of health services. How we perceive pain will continue to be influenced by and embedded in the technological, social and cultural context.

CHAPTER TWO

# Sociological Theory, Concepts and Pain

Most people are familiar with the idea of pain as a biomedical concept, and some will also be aware of the psychological components of pain, but the notion of pain as a subject of sociological analysis is not so well known. This is hardly surprising when you realise that sociologists themselves did not really begin to theorise pain and other issues of the body until very recently. Some sociologists would still argue that such enquiry is a form of 'sociological imperialism' (Strong, 1979), referring to the incorporation into sociology of a concept that most properly belongs in another discipline, in this case biomedicine. As sociology is such a broad discipline it is subject to territorial disputes between it and other social sciences, most notably psychology, but also social anthropology. It is easy to argue that sociology is concerned with the nature of society, psychologists with individuals and anthropologists with culture (the way that people live), but it is also easy to see how these things overlap. Society is made up of individuals, who are influenced by culture and by the dominant thinking in society, so the distinctions become blurred. In some ways a piece of research can be defined by the theoretical stance it adopts, e.g. a sociologist will build on previous work in that genre, but this may mean that very useful and informative literature from other disciplines does not become incorporated into the generation of knowledge. That said, there are also disputes *within* sociology about the nature of society, and the relative importance of structure and action (or agency).

Before we consider the question of what sociology is, and engage with some of the theories and concepts relevant to this

book, it may be useful to say what sociology is not. It is sometimes said that sociology is 'just common sense', that there
is nothing complex or difficult about explaining, for example,
pain, which is a physiological response to a stimulus, such as
an injury or a burn. However, our common-sense views tend
to arise from our experiences and from the world around us,
so that people from a different social class, or from different
parts of the world, may have a different common-sense view of
something. In reality, sociology seeks to look beyond what may
seem obvious or self-evident, and to question and challenge
what we may take for granted. If pain is a purely physiological
response, why don't we all react to the same degree of pain in
the same way? Why do health professionals treat some people
in pain with more credibility than others? Why do people interpret and make sense of pain differently within the context of
their lives? The ways in which sociologists seek to answer such
questions and challenge common-sense views will become
apparent throughout the book.

## Sociological traditions

Like any academic discipline sociology includes many different traditions and ways of viewing the world. This chapter
introduces some of these, but does not attempt to provide a
comprehensive introduction to sociological theory. Rather,
it comprises a brief discussion of those theories and concepts that have relevance for the following chapters, and that
are utilised by the studies which will be used as evidence or
illustration.

It could be argued that sociology has been undertaken for
hundreds, perhaps thousands, of years, but for our purposes
we can trace European sociology, and the first use of the word,
to nineteenth-century France and the social and economic
revolutions of the period. The philosopher Auguste Comte
(1798–1857) first used the word 'sociology' to define the scientific study of the social world, which he considered particularly

relevant to the emergence of industrial capitalism in Europe at the time (Comte, 1975). Sociology as a discipline developed at different rates in different parts of the world, depending on the degree of acceptance it was given by established disciplines, such as economics, and by the ability of sociologists to find academic space within universities. One result was that sociology developed and achieved respectability earlier in the United States than in Europe (Marsh et al., 2009).

The different traditions of sociology developed out of attempts to make sense of the move from agrarian to industrial society, urbanisation, the growth of waged labour, and the struggle for democracy. One of the most important distinctions in sociology is that between social structure and social action.

## Structuralist theories

*Consensus theories – Durkheim and Parsons*
Considered the 'founding father' of sociology, Emile Durkheim (1858–1917) was a consensus theorist in that he perceived the structures in society as the basis of social order and stability. Durkheim was concerned with how society maintained order and coherence in the face of massive social change, such as had occurred in France during the first half of the nineteenth century. He argued that society was a reality that was irreducible to its component parts, which could only be considered in relation to the whole. Social order within society could only be maintained by shared values and ties. In earlier eras, the traditional ties of feudalism and religion ('mechanical solidarity') had maintained social order, but these were no longer valid in post-industrial Europe. More complex societies with a division of labour and increasing individualism were problematic for social order, but Durkheim believed that a new social order would emerge based on 'organic solidarity', or the interdependence of economic ties (Giddens, 1971). Coherence is now maintained in society by regulation and constraints that are

accepted as legitimate by the population. So, for example, in today's societies most individuals accept the existence of speed limits, the school leaving age, or driving tests as necessary for society to function in an orderly way. There is a general consensus that these things benefit the smooth running of society, and they are not viewed as a restriction on individuals.

From the point of view of this volume, Durkheim's most relevant work is his book *Suicide* (1897). Durkheim viewed suicide, along with other phenomena, as a 'social fact'; that is, it exists in and of itself and outside of individual human action. In other words, people taking their own lives are not merely committing an individual act but are driven by social causes, even though these may not be apparent to the observer. Based on his analysis of suicide statistics in different societies, Durkheim produced a typology of suicide as follows:

- Egoistical suicide, which results from a lack of integration in society. A person may feel excluded from what is happening around them, as if they don't belong, are inadequate or worthless.
- Altruistic suicide, where a person feels they have a higher calling that means they must die for the greater good, as in the case of suicide bombers.
- Anomic suicide, which occurs during periods of social upheaval when the rules are no longer familiar and stable, and the person feels confused by and at odds with the changing social order, be it economic or personal (Durkheim, 1952).

In Chapter 7 we will consider these issues as they are reflected in emotional pain and suffering, but here it is worth mentioning an example of research that used Durkheim's concept of social integration to hypothesise that suicide rates in the USA would increase with decreases in per capita spending on public welfare. Using six data points in the years between 1960 and 1995, and controlling for variables such as levels of divorce, unemployment, sex ratio and race, it was found that suicide rates did increase with decreases in public welfare, and that the co-variable of divorce had the strongest and most persistent effect. However, the mechanism by which this occurred could not be established (Zimmerman, 2002).

*The sick role*
One of the first systematic, sociological accounts of health and illness was developed in the 1950s by Talcott Parsons. In his book *The Social System* (1951) Parsons argued that the structures of a society were organised in such a way as to produce the orderly functioning of that society. Health is essential for the functioning of society, and therefore illness is dysfunctional, or deviant, and needs to be understood within this context. So it is a requirement of society that illness be minimised, and managed within the context of cultural values and societal functioning. Within Western post-industrial societies, and increasingly also other types of social organisation, the role of sanctioning and legitimising sickness has been delegated to the medical profession. It is they who control the designation of sickness, and prevent social deviance on the part of those claiming to be sick.

Parsons developed the concept of the sick role to explain the conditions under which a person may be awarded the status of 'sick'. In their encounter, both the patient and the medical professional, usually a doctor, have rights and responsibilities. The patient is exempt from work and other normal duties, and is not held responsible for their condition. In return they must want to recover and seek competent technical help to do so. The doctor must act to the best of his or her professional ability and in the best interests of the patients; in return the doctor has the exclusive right of access to the body and to privileged information. It is through the conferment of this temporary function that order in society is not disrupted by illness (Parsons, 1951). Perhaps due to the fact that functionalist theories have fallen out of favour, research on pain and painful conditions rarely takes a functionalist stance. However, in many of the studies cited in this book, particularly those examining unexplained symptoms and contested disease, you will find the struggle to gain access to the sick role either overtly expressed or implied. Parsons' legacy 'is a rich one that lives on within and beyond the sociology of health and illness' (Williams, 2005: 140).

*Criticisms of consensus theories*
Consensus theorists in general have been criticised for focusing excessively on the positive aspects of societal functioning, assuming agreement about how societies should be organised, and ignoring conflict. So, for example, it is argued that professionals will always act altruistically in the interests of their client group and not for self-interest or personal gain. In Chapter 8, however, we will see that health professionals sometimes have attitudes and values that do not coincide with the interests of patients. In particular, Parsons has also been accused of failing to account for diversity – age, ethnicity and gender, for example – and in Chapter 4 we will discuss how these variables influence the experience and treatment of pain. Although Parsons did acknowledge the diversity of illness and the capacity to recover, the strongest criticism of the idea of the sick role has been its failure to account for long-term illness, in which we must include chronic pain. The value of Parsons' work, however, lies in its identifying for the first time health and illness as suitable topics for sociological investigation.

*Conflict theorists – Karl Marx and neo-Marxists*
As the label would suggest, conflict theorists reject the idea of the organisation of society being conducted by consensus and argue that society is defined by conflict. Karl Marx (1818–83), like Durkheim, lived through a period of social upheaval – in his native Prussia, and also in France – but it was his interest in economic theory that led to his major works on the capitalist system of production. During the nineteenth century the production of goods moved from basically small-scale industry serving local populations to large-scale factory production

in urban conurbations, with a division of labour based on the completion of specific tasks. Observing nineteenth-century industry, Marx concluded that capitalist society was formed of two classes that were dialectically opposed – those who owned the means of production and those who worked for them. Workers sell their labour, but do not receive its full value, the surplus being taken by the owners of the productive unit as profit (Giddens, 1971). In this way, Marx argued, capitalism will always exploit labour. The owners of capital also decide *what* goods get produced, and will ensure that wages are just high enough to enable workers to buy them, so that profits continue. As more goods and services are commodified (given a monetary value so that they can be bought and sold), so capitalism expands. Turning that argument around, for capitalist production to expand, more goods and services need to be commodified.

Marx was, of course, writing before the development of modern healthcare systems, but neo-Marxist writers, such as Vincente Navarro and John McKinley, have used Marxist theory to examine the organisation of healthcare and the role of the medical profession (see, for example, Navarro, 1981). As both write about the US healthcare system, which is based on the free market, it could be argued that their ideas are not transferable to more collectivist systems, but much of their work has wider resonance. Navarro also includes within his edited volumes critiques of other Western healthcare systems (see, for example, Navarro, 2004). Neo-Marxist writers acknowledge the increasing involvement of the state in healthcare, but argue that this is done to protect the capitalist system and the private sector. For example, if workers are sick or injured they cannot contribute to the production of goods, so it is in the interest of capital that they are treated and returned to work. It is viewed as no accident that the areas of healthcare that are underfunded and of low status – care of the elderly, learning disability and long-term mental ill health – affect those who are less active economically. Doctors legitimise illness not for the smooth functioning of society, as functionalists maintain, but in the interests of the capitalist system (McKinley, 1977). Health professionals, it is argued, also collude with capitalism to hide the real causes of ill health (poverty, pollution, etc.) by focusing on individual causes (biomedical and lifestyle).

Neo-Marxists also point to the commodification of health-care in the increase in pharmaceutical products and the massive profits made by the industry, similarly in the growth in cosmetic surgery and other lifestyle treatments. Are these products developed out of medical need or in order to increase profit? Capitalism also benefits from the lack of controls on harmful products such as alcohol, tobacco and sugar, which cause ill health but are produced by rich and powerful corporations that can lobby and influence government policy.

Critiques of Marxist and neo-Marxist theory claim that its emphasis on economic determinants ignores other aspects of social relationships, such as family, that constitute societal structure. They also point out that Marx's predictions for the overthrow of capitalism have not been borne out, and other events unforeseen by Marx, such as two world wars, have instead shored up the status quo.

## Social action theories

Both consensus and conflict structural theories have been criti-cised for focusing purely on the structures of society to explain its organisation (macrosociology), and so ignoring agency or social action. Social action theorists claim that individuals do not merely respond to their situation within society but pos-sess volition, and their values and motives can influence their actions (microsociology).

Max Weber (1864–1920) was very complex in his thinking about society and the way people behave in a given situation, such that there is no one grand theory that encapsulates the varying facets of his work. He disagreed with Marx's emphasis on conflict to explain the nature of society, and argued that people are sentient and reasoning beings who attach meaning to their actions, and that sociologists need to acknowledge this. So a sociological analysis, according to Weber, needs to be grounded in the meanings that people give to their actions within their social setting. In the chapters that follow a recurring theme is how people make sense of pain within the context of their lives, and how this influences the ways in which they manage it. To describe his sociological approach, Weber used the term *verstehen*, which may be translated as the empathetic understanding of human action, that is, attempting to understand it from the point of view of the actor (Giddens, 1971). Of course that begs the question of how a sociologist can be certain that they have correctly interpreted the meanings that others place on their behaviour. Weber suggested that there were four basic categories of action (what he called 'ideal types') that could act as a standard of classification against which behaviours could be measured. These are:

- Traditional action, influenced by custom and habit.
- Affective action, guided by emotions.
- Value-rational action, involving deeply held values and morals.
- Technical-rational action, in which rational means are chosen, with regards to consequences. (Marsh et al., 2009).

It is the last of these that Weber perceived as pre-eminent in modern society, and the most amenable to sociological investigation.

Weber also classified types of authority, which he saw as necessary for societies to exist. Traditional authority is feudal and founded on authority being possessed as a right by some within a society. Bureaucratic authority is based on formal rules and legal norms. Charismatic authority is achieved by the force of personality and persuasiveness of a person to inspire others to follow. Such people tend to be anti-bureaucratic and anti-tradition. For example, it has been argued by James and Field (1992) that the rise of the hospice movement for end-of-life care was the result of the reforming zeal of a charismatic person, Cicely Saunders, although as it grew it inevitably became more routinised and bureaucratic (see Chapter 4).

## Interpretive theories

Interpretive approaches in sociology focus on human inter-action, and the influence on an individual's behaviour of the reactions of those around them. Some of the most insightful research on pain has used this approach to explore the experi-ence of pain and how people interpret and make sense of what is happening to them, or how that experience impacts on a carer. The researcher's role here is to attempt to see the world from the perspective of the patient or the carer, not to analyse their experience using some abstract external theory. In most of the cases to be presented in this book, pain is perceived neg-atively by the sufferer, but one study that used an interpretive approach to explore the meaning of resilience to people with chronic pain found that individuals could find positive ways to control both their pain and their lives. Resilience was a journey rather than a state of mind, but the participants in the study described how they had learned to accept their pain and look for the positives in life (West et al., 2012).

*Symbolic interactionism*
Out of Weber's theories of meaning and action microsocio-logical approaches to analysing behaviour were developed, in particular by the Chicago School, which became synonymous with symbolic interactionism following its ethnographic (i.e. based on observation) study of life in the rapidly changing and expanding city of Chicago. Symbolic interactionism grew out of the work of George H. Mead (1863–1931) on the develop-ment of the self, and the term was first used by his student Herbert Blumer (1900–87) (see Blumer, 1969). With the dominance of macrosociology in the 1950s, '60s and '70s, micro approaches fell out of favour, but the move towards

postmodern thinking towards the end of the twentieth century led to greater emphasis on relativism and a blurring of traditional boundaries.

Symbolic interactionists are concerned with the meanings that people impose on behaviour and events. These are subjective, rather than based on what is objectively thought to be true. So the way that people behave is based on what they believe, on how they interpret themselves and others, and these interpretations form the basis of social relationships. Meanings are not fixed or bounded, but may be modified or developed by further experience, new interactions or different situations (Plummer, 1996). The majority of research in this tradition is qualitative, using ethnographic approaches which record and analyse in-depth descriptions of life and experience. This is usually conducted by observation, and unstructured or semi-structured interviews or focus groups, in which participants are able to introduce topics of importance to them, and interact with the researcher, rather than just answer set questions.

Critics of symbolic interactionism accuse it of being unsystematic, and reject the tools of qualitative research as ungeneralisable. It is also said to ignore wider social factors that influence people's behaviour. However, the researcher using this approach aims to gain insight and understanding, rather than to generalise.

In considering research on pain we can contrast quantitative research, which tends to utilise validated pain-measurement scales such as the McGill Pain Questionnaire, with qualitative interactionist research on pain, many examples of which will be found in the following chapters. Using a number of descriptors of pain, the McGill scale (discussed further in Chapter 4) provides a numerical value for an individual's pain, which can be used before and after an intervention to measure improvement or deterioration. It can also be used to compare the pain of people suffering from the same condition, and produce an average over a large group. It will not tell you, however, how that pain is experienced, what it feels like, or how it impacts on people's lives and relationships. For that, participants need to be given the opportunity to impart their pain in their own way.

## Erving Goffman and stigma

Erving Goffman (1922–82) did not see himself as a symbolic interactionist, but his work was heavily influenced by Blumer as well as others from that tradition. The phrase that is often associated with Goffman's work is 'all the world's a stage', from Shakespeare's *As You Like It*, because he saw people as acting out roles, negotiating with others, and generally behaving as if in a theatrical play. So the same individual may be a strict employer, an indulgent parent, and a loyal friend. We all have many parts in the play and different ideas about how to act in each; and we make decisions on how to play the part based on the impression we wish to create. Later in the book we will look at how patients with unexplained pain work at creating the 'right' tone when interacting with medical staff in order to be perceived as credible (Werner and Malterud, 2003).

Goffman's work on stigma is particularly relevant to the experience of pain, as it relates to a focus on perceptions rather than the level of pain. In his book *Stigma: Notes on the Management of a Spoiled Identity* (1968) Goffman argues that stigma is a discrediting label that marks someone out as different, can change the way that individual is viewed, and can 'spoil' their identity. There are, according to his theory, two types of stigmatising condition: those that are clearly visible such as skin diseases or cerebral palsy, which he calls discrediting, and those that can be hidden, such as diabetes, or kidney disease. The latter are discreditable conditions as they have the potential to be discrediting but the individual experiencing them may choose not to disclose their condition to others. For example, women suffering from vaginitis may avoid disclosure or only disclose selectively, due to shame about experiencing vaginal symptoms, and the association with bodily fluids (Karasz and Anderson, 2003). Discreditable conditions may have the potential to become discrediting, for example if a person living with epilepsy has a seizure in a public place. They may then be viewed differently by others, as the label of 'epileptic' is added to their list of attributes. Apart from visibility, a condition may be stigmatised because of its association with negative attributes, such as sexual promiscuity (HIV) or malingering (back pain). This may lead to 'enacted stigma', where the stigmatising condition leads to actual discrimination. On the other hand, felt stigma causes feelings of shame in the absence of any negative experience.

Finally, 'courtesy stigma' is the feeling of stigma felt by those around someone with a stigmatised condition, such as the carer of a person with learning disability (Goffman, 1968). More recently, Scambler and Hopkins (1986) have differentiated between stigma and deviance, terms that have been used interchangeably. Stigma evokes feelings of shame within an individual whereas deviance implies blame, either for contracting the disease itself or for shortcomings in the way it is dealt with. Many studies on pain have addressed the notion of stigma, and it is often raised by participants themselves as something that negatively affects their lives. Some of this work will be explored in later chapters, in particular in relation to women's reproductive health. Women experiencing infertility speak of stigmatising feelings of shame, guilt and inadequacy, and of being abnormal and incomplete (Whiteford and Gonzalez, 1995). They also describe the spoiled identity of infertility, with one woman commenting: 'I try not to let myself believe that I'm not as great of [sic] a person as I would be if I had a child. [But] I think of myself as a failure' (Whiteford and Gonzalez, 1995: 33).

## Feminist theories

Most feminist theory is based on the idea that patriarchy – a system of male domination of women – is the oldest, most widely experienced and most persistent form of discrimination. From that basic starting point, however, a diverse set of perspectives follows, covering a broad political spectrum, which it is beyond the scope of this volume to cover. However, feminist thought is often said to comprise three waves (Marsh et al., 2009). The first wave, starting from around the end of the eighteenth century, was concerned with achieving the same rights for women as for men, for example property rights, voting rights, or entry into education and the professions. By the time of the second wave, during the 1960s and '70s, many of the battles around entitlement had been won and the issues moved on to equal pay and other employment rights, and greater representation in public life. Around this time feminists rejected the domestic and reproductive roles as defining women, arguing that while there are biological differences between men and women, social roles and norms are socially and historically constructed, and furthermore constructed in a way that is advantageous to men. Third-wave feminism, beginning around the 1990s, moves away from rigid notions of gender and equality and embraces the relativism of postmodernism mentioned above. In some ways it addresses criticisms to second-wave feminism, in particular that it essentialised sex and gender and focused on both from the perspective of white, middle-class women. Third-wave feminism incorporates multiple and related issues of disadvantage, such as race, age, disability, sexuality and class, and moves towards more fluid ideas of sex and gender. It has also noted that simply 'adding women' to public life did not alter power relations, but merely added a second or even third shift to their domestic and caring roles (Marsh et al., 2009).

Feminist writing on pain has been very much concerned with gendered notions of pain, and the trivialising and psychologising of women's pain in particular. It has also addressed the clinical encounter and the way that women may feel disempowered and disbelieved in consultations with health professionals. It has, however, been argued that this focus on women as research participants has served to reinforce the myth of women as weak and in need of male attention (Bradby,

2012). Nevertheless, while women are the main users of healthcare, and the vast majority of formal and informal carers are women, they still lack power within the healthcare sphere.

## Foucault and power

'Knowledge is power' is a much-repeated phrase. For Michel Foucault (1926–84), whose concept of the clinical gaze was addressed in Chapter 1, power is control over the production of knowledge, and the two are therefore inextricably linked (Rabinow, 1991). Foucault moves beyond both structural theories of power, such as Marxism, and social action theory, to conceptualise power as something that is produced rather than possessed. The way in which language is used, or 'discourse', conveys a specific meaning which in turn leads to a body of knowledge that defines what is normal and therefore what is abnormal and deviant. Discourse frames the way we view the event or object being described, and its labels, as we shall see throughout this book, impact on the way in which patients are perceived, and can influence the treatment they receive. Consider this simple example – a patient in a hospital ward is described by a health professional thus: 'This is Mrs Smith. She is fit to go home and is blocking a bed.' Conversely it could be phrased: 'This is Mrs Smith. She is fit to go home, but her discharge and follow-up care has not been organised.' The first phrasing implies that Mrs Smith is at fault, which may impact on her subsequent care, yet she is powerless to change the perception of herself in the eyes of her carers. This phrasing also deflects blame away from the organisation that has failed to organise her care.

The use of discourse to create a particular image may be deliberate or unthinking, but it is frequently used to construct a particular version of 'truth'. Social reality, then, is not some fixed entity, but depends on our ways of defining the social world. Professional power is reinforced by the use of esoteric knowledge and technical language to exclude the uninitiated, and many writers in this area have taken a Foucauldian stance in addressing doctor–patient interactions, as we shall explore in Chapter 8. For example, Sarah Nettleton has used Foucault's notion of the gaze and his conception of power to explore pain and the associated fear of dental procedures. She argues that in the past dental pain was viewed as existing purely in the mouth of the patient, and therefore as something to be controlled by analgesics administered by the dentist. This perception shifted over time to include the psychological and emotional states of the patient, in particular their fear. Later this fear was perceived to be located in 'a psychological space, a region between the mind and the mouth' (Nettleton, 1989: 1188), in which a trusting and cooperative patient facilitates the dentist's work. In addressing pain and fear, dentistry could extend its gaze to those whose fear of pain results in them not attending for dental check-ups. Nettleton concludes that shifting power relationships are not just the result of the political or professional manoeuvrings of a particular group, but are more subtle. This is consistent with the findings of Arney and Neill around pain in childbirth. These authors argued that, following the Second World War, and in response to the challenge of the natural childbirth movement, obstetrics reformulated its understanding of pain during labour. Perceptions shifted from seeing pain as something that needed to be obliterated in order to facilitate the work of the obstetrician, to pain as something to be worked with and managed, taking into account the subjectivity of the birthing woman (Arney and Neill, 1982). So rather than relinquish power over pain control, or reject the subjective wishes of the woman, obstetrics incorporated them and 'recaptured pain, relocated it so that it stood outside women, between them and the optimal childbirth experience which could be achieved only with obstetrics' managerial assistance' (Arney and Neill, 1982: 19). This increasing power of obstetricians, incidentally, cannot be divorced from the decline of the midwife over the early part of the twentieth century (see van Teijlingen, 2015).

Despite the discussion above, Foucault did not view discursive power in purely negative terms, but saw it as also having the potential to be transformative, opening us up to new ideas and ways of thinking (see Rabinow, 1991).

## Sociology of the body

Earlier in this chapter it was noted that, traditionally, bodily functions and experiences were not generally considered relevant topics for sociological investigation, but were thought to belong in positivist disciplines concerned with individuals rather than structures, such as biomedicine and psychology. The task of sociology was to move beyond individualism, with its connotations of victim-blaming, in order to understand structural problems. Beginning in the 1980s, this approach was challenged by, among others, writers on disability (Frank, 1990). Some of the arguments made for including the body within a sociology of disability are illustrative of the debate over structure and action (or agency) more generally.

Traditionally disability was seen as a biomedical problem, and the response of health services was to enable the individual to adapt and adjust. This individualistic approach began to be challenged, mainly by disabled activists themselves. Sociologists such as Michael Oliver and Colin Barnes argued that people are not disabled by an impairment such as spina bifida, but by the structures of society that exclude and discriminate against them (Oliver and Barnes, 2012). The social model of disability highlights the barriers faced by disabled people in living their lives and engaging in social, economic and political activity.

This approach has been criticised by other disabled writers, such as Liz Crow (1996), who argues that the social model of disability fails to deal with physical symptoms, such as pain, which impact on a person's life and restrict their ability to undertake activities. She adds that disability and impairment cannot be understood in isolation, but are the external and internal constituent parts of a disabled person's experience. Hughes and Paterson state that:

> The distinction between disability and impairment de-medicalises disability, but simultaneously leaves the impaired body in the exclusive jurisdiction of medical hermeneutics. While a sociology of the body seeks to challenge the medical monopoly over knowledge about the body, the social model of disability concedes it. (1997: 330)

As Williams (2000) argues, the sociology of the body and the sociology of disability are diverging, with the former moving towards the problem of embodiment and the latter away from it. Shakespeare (2006) has called the division between impairment and disability a false dualism, as impairment is social, and disability includes impairment. Bodily experiences are social experiences.

Like Williams, Nettleton (2006a), among others, prefers to focus on embodiment, that is, the experience of living in a body, rather than its physical attributes, and this approach is particularly useful in thinking about the reality of living in a body with pain. So whereas a biomedical approach tends to view the body as a machine, in which things go wrong that can be fixed by health professionals (see also Chapter 8), embodiment approaches analyse bodies that become difficult to live in (e.g. due to illness) and therefore also difficult to ignore. Our body, then, is something we have and also something we are. A number of the women with vaginitis who took part in a study by Alison Karasz and Matthew Anderson (see above) reported feeling that even a healthy vagina was unclean, and that any infection was a sign of promiscuity or was sexually transmitted. Other women felt that a 'normal' vagina should have some, but not a lot of secretions. The embodied stories the women told differed from the dominant medical view of vaginitis as a self-limiting, not very serious infection that is amenable to antibiotics (Karasz and Anderson, 2003).

Another factor in the acknowledgement of the body as a relevant topic for sociological examination has been the increasing surveillance of the body in more reductionist ways, for example by antenatal scanning for foetal abnormality, mammography to detect breast cancer, or genetic testing, all of which open up the body to ever more scrutiny. Accepting such surveillance has become a technological imperative, the moral choice in accepting responsibility in caring for the body (Denny, 2015). Sociology has drawn attention to the essentialist nature of this approach and the uncritical way in which the technology has been introduced.

In short, a sociology of the body, or of embodiment, seeks to engage in problems such as pain using a non-medicalised approach, one that seeks to unpack and question both the inner workings of the body and the external responses to them. It also acknowledges the diversity of interest, in that a teenager with spina bifida, a middle-aged man with obstructive airway disease, and an elderly person with osteoarthritis represent very different faces of disability needs and experience.

## Summary

Durkheim, Marx and Weber are considered the founding thinkers of sociology. Whereas Durkheim and Marx focused on social structures, Weber introduced the idea of social actors being influential in social change and provided a bridge between structural and interpretive theories. Symbolic interactionists, on the other hand, were concerned with small-scale interactions and the meanings placed on them. More recently, sociologists have sought to incorporate the body into sociological thinking, and to give voice to individual experience and the meanings people attach to it. In later chapters, both macro- and micro-level sociology will be seen to play a part in the interpretation of pain. For example, in Chapter 5, on diversity, social action will frequently be situated within a structural framework.

From the very different sociological perspectives introduced in this chapter it can be seen that sociology is a very broad church, with many competing explanations of phenomena and events. As C. Wright Mills (1970) argued, the purpose of sociology is to examine the complex relationship between the individual and society. Structures such as social class and gender may be influential in the experience of pain, and how pain is interpreted by the sufferer, their health professionals, and their friends and family will also affect the experience. Much recent sociological work, such as that found in sociology of the body, rejects the dichotomous positioning of structural and action theories and instead views society as more complex and relational. Sociology aims to make people challenge the ideas they have previously 'taken for granted', their 'common-sense' view of the world. Its theories and concepts can assist us in understanding the different perspectives from which events and phenomena can be interpreted, and views that diverge from our own. It is one of the tools in the toolkit we use to understand and make sense of the world.

# CHAPTER THREE

# The Experience of Pain

In her book *The C Word*, about the experience of living with cancer and its treatments (surgery, radiotherapy, chemotherapy), Lisa Lynch relates an occasion when 'Always-Right Breast Nurse' (A-RBN) asked her to speak to another patient who was about to undergo mastectomy and chemotherapy:

> A-RBN chipped in 'Chemo wasn't quite as bad as you'd expected it to be was it, Lisa?' Uncomfortable pause. I wanted to answer 'No, it was a damn fucking sight worse', but held back for the sake of the chemotherapy novice before me.
> I was confused as to why Always-Right Breast Nurse had said that . . .
> But then it dawned on me. For the first time I realised that, actually, I'd always made a point of playing down the effects of chemo to Smiley Surgeon and Always-Right Breast Nurse. I hadn't lied about it per se; I'd just never given them the full picture. And, having only ever seen them in my chemo 'good weeks', I could get away with it, too. (Lynch, 2015: 266)

This extract provides an example of how public and private accounts of illness may differ. Health professionals tend to see a snapshot of people during clinic visits or during treatment. They cannot know how illness impacts on people's lives outside of these encounters, unless the individual chooses (and gets the opportunity) to tell them. For Lisa her private experience of chemotherapy was one of hallucinations, constipation, aching bones and vomiting, but the public face that she chose to present to her doctors was of a smiling, well-dressed young woman who was positive and coping well. In order to understand these private accounts we need to pay attention to experiences such as these, which are increasingly found not by traditional means, such as in research findings published in books and journal articles, but on the internet in blogs or self-help sites (*The C Word* was originally a blog). This chapter is concerned with how the person in pain interprets and conveys their experience to others.

Research which aims to gain insight into a phenomenon such as pain will frequently use a narrative or storytelling approach that allows the participant to recount their experience in a way that gives prominence to issues that are meaningful to them. This approach has been criticised as lacking in analysis and as taking place in a social vacuum (and of course a blog records one person's experience at one period in time). But, as we discussed in Chapter 2, much of sociology is concerned with understanding the way people experience and make sense of their world, rather than making generalisations that apply to whole populations. Arthur Frank, in writing of his own periods of ill health, comments that being a patient – that is, receiving medical treatment in a healthcare facility – was only part of a life in which being ill remained constantly present. During periods of hospitalisation, being a patient can dominate one's life, but for much of the time people with long-term illness and pain are not patients under the gaze of health professionals, but are engaged in incorporating pain into their day-to-day lives. People tell stories to remind others who suffer from the same condition (for example, fellow sufferers of chronic low back pain) what it is that they share, and to give those who do not share it a glimpse of what it is like to live with that condition (Frank, 2000).

As well as exploring the experience of pain using narrative accounts we will also consider work demonstrating how pain caused by long-term illness can disrupt an individual's identity and biography. A consideration of a very specific aspect of pain, the experience of torture, will follow. Because of its enduring nature, long-term pain has been the focus of much sociological enquiry, but the issues around acute pain will also feature in this chapter.

## Illness narrative

Hydén (1997) argues that the speech of patients has a somewhat ambiguous status in biomedicine. We saw in Chapter 1 how the patient's narrative became less influential as medicine became more reductionist and biochemical tests and imaging played a far more important role in diagnosis. 'How patients spoke about their ills, symptoms and problems was regarded at best as a pale reflection of the language of organs and tissues' (Hydén, 1997: 48); in other words the patient's subjective story is treated as less reliable than supposedly objective testing. Hydén implicates social scientists before the late 1980s in this version of social reality, with their use of biomedical definitions as a starting point for study, and their linking of patient perspectives to this with terms such as 'illness behaviour' or 'lay perspective', which imply something outside of, rather than integral to, the practice of 'real' medicine. Although this approach has been challenged, you will notice throughout this book that the ubiquity of biomedical definitions is hard to avoid; but it is important to note that this approach is only one lens through which to view ideas of health and illness. According to Hydén, the opportunity to move beyond this biomedical hegemony came with the distinctions between 'illness' and 'disease' and between illness and the suffering that accompanies it. The way was thus open for narrative to become a legitimate area of sociological research. Narrative concerns not only what people say but how they say it, how it is ordered, and the emphasis put on various parts of it. Narratives are important in the study of long-term illness as a means of understanding how people attempt to deal with their lives and the problems of identity that their illness brings (Hydén, 1997). An illness narrative is 'a story the patient tells, and significant others retell, to give coherence to the distinctive events and long-term course of suffering' (Kleinman, 1988: 49). Narratives are the method by which people shape and give voice to their suffering (this aspect of narrative will be addressed in Chapter 8).

There are various ways of viewing illness narrative (see, for example, Robinson, 1988; Williams, 1984), but here we will consider those of Hydén (1997) and Frank (1995). It is probably useful here to distinguish between 'narrative' and 'story', although Frank (2000) admits he often uses the terms interchangeably. However, as he also notes, people do not 'tell narratives', they tell stories. 'Narrative' implies the structure underpinning the story, but in focusing on such structures an interpreter may leave unexamined what is most important to the storyteller. On the other hand, Bury (2001) warns against accepting narratives as self-evident, arguing that it is the responsibility of the researcher to interpret and contextualise narrative, to ask 'why was that story told in that way'. There is an implied tension here between maintaining the integrity of the story and the interpretive responsibility of the researcher, a tension that sociologists using narrative approaches seek to manage.

Frank (1995) classifies three types of illness narrative: restitution, quest and chaos. The restitution narrative is one we are all familiar with, when we move from a normal healthy state to one of temporary illness, and then, following a passage of time and perhaps some treatment, we are again restored to health and move on. Restitution stories only work, however, for as long as the body is restorable; when someone's illness becomes chronic or terminal then other stories have to be prepared.

In the quest narrative illness is a journey from the previous life to a new normal; it is accepted and the experience of pain, the hopes and fears of the sufferer, are shared in the hope of gaining insight. Restitution may or may not eventually be possible. The quest narrative provides greater opportunity for the ill to tell their story, and most published illness stories are quest narratives. A Google search of any self-help health charity or national newspaper will elicit many quest narratives, often using the language and metaphors of war – 'my battle against cancer', 'a struggle against alcoholism', 'fighting

depression' – where the heroic sufferer confronts the challenge of their illness, and may even find some positive aspects
in the experience.

The chaos narrative lacks the reflection of the previous narrative types, as in this situation illness is not characterised as
a sequence of events. The plot of a chaos narrative is not a
linear progression, but moves in an unpredictable way. No one
has control, neither the storyteller nor the health professionals
who cannot cure the disease. To this extent chaos is actually
an anti-narrative. There may be periods of respite in between
periods of extreme pain, but the future is uncertain. The tell-
ers of chaos narratives are the Wounded Storytellers referred
to in the title of Frank's book (1995). Later, Frank writes that
chronic pain creates a chaos narrative, where the body seems
to be turning against itself:

> How the present troubles began is often forgotten – a time
> before illness and pain becomes hard to remember – and no
> end is in sight. In this chaos anti-narrative, a feedback loop
> connects the pain that seems to come from within the body
> to the social relationships that seem outside the body. Pain
> informs how people experience others around them, and
> those others affect the level of pain. (2005: 291)

Hydén argues that Frank's typology of narrative is based on a
meta-analysis (chaos, quest and restitution), whereas he is concerned with the relationship between narrator, narrative and
illness. This again results in three types of illness narrative:

*Illness as narrative.* This is probably the type most familiar to
most people. Here, narrator, narrative and illness are one; the
narrative is the story through which the individual expresses
and articulates their experience of illness. Symptoms and
consequences are integrated into a new whole, which in turn
forms part of a new social reality.

*Narrative about illness.* This is narrative about the illness
rather than the individual, and is used by health professionals
to talk about the illness, to gain information in order to reach
a diagnosis and decide on treatment. These narratives are

important in formulating and conveying clinical knowledge, both to patients and to colleagues.

*Narrative as illness.* This reflects instances where the inability to articulate or to form a narrative is a crucial part of the illness itself, as in brain injury, or the exclusion of certain parts of the past from memory.

## Examples of illness narratives

Narratives may have several uses in respect of an individual's relationship with others and in constructing social realities (Hydén, 1997: 55). Through narrative an illness world may be constructed; Hydén gives the example of a person in chronic pain using narratives to give a starting point to the pain, including any precipitating factors, and to provide small examples of the everyday consequences and limitations posed by the pain. Through narrative individuals can reconstruct their personal identity, and reorder their life history, incorporating their past life within the new reality in order to maintain the connection. Narratives can be a medium for discussing the 'why me?', 'why now?' questions to which many people seek the answer, and can build upon cultural ideas of illness causation. Narratives may also transform the individual experience of illness into a collective one, so someone with chronic pelvic pain will identify with others suffering from the same condition, and view themselves as part of a social community. This has been facilitated in recent times by the proliferation of online self-help groups and blogs (see above), where narratives are used to compare symptoms and treatments, and to offer advice on pain management and dealing with health professionals.

We can illustrate the value of narrative to our understanding of living with pain by considering two quite different conditions that have the experience of pain as a common factor: fibromyalgia and cancer.

Fibromyalgia is a long-term condition that will be explored in more detail in Chapter 6, as there are aspects of it that make it contested. Here we are interested in a study of the experience of women with fibromyalgia using stories to explore their daily lives. In a Norwegian study, Råheim and Håland (2006) interviewed twelve women and developed three typologies to encapsulate their stories, categorising each story into one of these types. One story from each category was presented in the research findings, in order to delve deeper into the meaning of fibromyalgia in the women's lives. Each typology revolves around the treacherous body, which was the common thread between them. The first group of women are represented by Maren (all the women were given pseudonyms), and are described as being powerless, at the mercy of the treacherous body. Maren tells of her struggle to get out of bed:

> It takes ages to get out of bed and into the bathroom. It is like moving mountains. I'm so extremely stiff, and the pain is just unbearable. It's just pain and pain! I don't look into the mirror, I don't care about dressing. I am just thinking: how on earth am I going to make it up the stairs. (Råheim and Håland, 2006: 747)

Agnete represents the second category, described as trying to escape the treacherous body, but she also demonstrates ambivalence. Although she had felt she had some control and had worked out ways of coping, these broke down on the birth of a new baby. But as she and her husband had got through bad times before, she also displayed ambivalence towards her situation.

The third category is that of coping with the treacherous body. Esther works full time and has four children. She has routines that help her avoid pain, and strategies to cope with it. She fights with her body and not against it, although doing so takes all of her strength.

A qualitative study with people suffering from cancer focused on why, despite being in considerable pain, they consistently took fewer analgesics than prescribed. Participants wove their experiences, beliefs and concerns into personal narratives, which the authors labelled 'pain management

autobiographies' (Schumacher et al., 2002: 127). One participant, Margaret, was concerned about addiction and for that
reason waited until her pain was severe before taking the analgesic. She commented:

> There is a reason why addiction is a (concern) – I had a severe
> neck and shoulder injury and for several years was on (a
> mild opioid). I remember, as God is my judge, I remember
> although they swore I didn't that I asked them at least 3 or 4
> times 'Are you sure I should be taking so much medication?'
> It would be like 1 (dose) in the morning, 1 (dose) in the after-
> noon, and 1 (dose) in the evening, so it was like 3 (doses) a day.
> Some days it was less than that. Some days I took none. After
> a period of about 3 years, my doctor decided I had become
> addicted, and I needed to go to the pain clinic where I would
> be weaned off medication totally. They didn't deny that I had
> the injury, they didn't deny that I had pain, but they said I had
> to quote – unquote 'learn how to live with it without medica-
> tion'. (Schumacher et al., 2002: 127–8)

This and other aspects of Margaret's narrative graphically illustrate the complex relationship between her past experience of
managing non-cancer pain, and her current feelings towards,
and management of, cancer pain. Such multiple threads of
experience were characteristic of the biographies obtained in
the study, and arose spontaneously from participants.

In these studies women's stories and the meanings they
placed on them were interpreted and reported by researchers,
who nevertheless gave primacy to what the women said during
interviews, and the way in which they interpreted and made
sense of their lives. There is also a history, beginning in the
1970s, of sociologists using their own experience of illness to
present an autobiographical account from a sociological perspective (see, for example, Roth, 1963; Jobling, 1988; Frank,
1991). Mildred Blaxter (2009) graphically describes her journey towards a diagnosis of lung cancer. As more diagnostic
tests were undertaken, the images created (visual images
such as scans and X-rays, as well as the reports and medical
records into which the results were distilled) began to take

precedence over the patient history and symptoms, render-
ing Mildred herself invisible and disembodied. However, she
notes that the problem was not the images themselves, which
could in fact be informative, but rather the complex system
in which the doctors (those ordering the biomedical tests and
interpreting the results) worked. The result is that 'images
and records appear to create and control both medical practice and the patient's medical experience' (Blaxter, 2009: 776).
Christopher Adamson kept a detailed diary in order to record
his experience of inflammatory bowel disease (IBD) and avascular necrosis (AVN), and the treatments he received, which
he describes as (eventually) a restitution story (Adamson,
1997). His narrative provides a graphic account of a long and
complicated illness trajectory, which revolved around existential and clinical uncertainty. Two of the issues raised by these
autobiographies – uncertainty and the value of visual imaging
– are further explored in Chapter 6.

Narrative research has become an important tool in qualitative research for allowing participants to tell their stories,
and to set them in a social context, embedded in the totality of
their lives. Although narratives have most often been utilised
to gain insight into the experience of long-term illness or pain,
they can also be used to explore what it is like to live with and/
or care for someone in pain, and this aspect will be explored
further in the next chapter.

## Biographical disruption

The concept of biographical disruption was first introduced
by Mike Bury in 1982, and has been an enduring feature of
research into long-term illness and pain since then. In the
course of his research with people living with rheumatoid
arthritis (RA), Bury noticed that the onset of chronic illness
constitutes a particular type of disruptive event. The life and
future that an individual has assumed and planned for needs
to be rethought; as Arthur Frank later put it, writing about his

own illness: '[s]erious illness is a loss of "the destination map" that had previously guided the ill person's life: ill people have to learn "to think differently"' (1995: 1). Chronic illness also brings pain, suffering and death into sharp relief, issues that are normally only thought about remotely in the distant future, or as affecting others (Bury, 1997). Biographical disruption not only describes what is happening, but also provides an analytical focus for the process of living with a long-term illness, moving on from the study of the problems people face in incorporating their responses to such illnesses.

As chronic illness unfolds, three aspects of disruption may be observed. First, the disruption of taken-for-granted assumptions and behaviours – the 'what is going on here?' questions that accompany an attention to bodily states not normally brought into consciousness. Second, a fundamental rethink of the person's biography and self-identity is brought about by the disruption of normal explanatory systems and social relationships. Finally, the response to such disruption involves the mobilisation of resources in light of the altered circumstances (Bury, 1982). In other words, the life that was expected is no longer possible due to the illness, and a new life plan has to be formulated and accommodated. As with many long-term illnesses, the early signs of RA are not dramatic but emerge gradually, and may at first be seen as no more than an inconvenience. Eventually the pain, stiffness and deformed joints become too much to ignore. RA is particularly problematic in that it affects relatively young people (the majority of Bury's participants being under fifty-five), and yet arthritis more generally is seen as a disease of older people, leading younger individuals to view themselves as ageing prematurely. So instead of an anticipated straightforward trajectory of life they are forced to shift their expectations of the future and of social relationships. Later Bury argued that while earlier sociological work on chronic illness had been concerned with the problems people faced, the focus on biographical disruption explores their responses to those problems and enables the meaning of their illness to be situated in a temporal and life-course context. (Bury, 1991). Interpretive approaches to chronic illness highlight the changes that occur over time, and the positive responses of individuals to the negative effects of symptoms and treatments.

Two types of meaning are involved in the onset of chronic illness. The first involves the consequences of the initial experience and the persistence of symptoms for practical and social functioning. This may be experienced as a growing awareness of the severity of symptoms and their effects on daily activities and social relationships, which leads to the second type of meaning, the significance of the illness. The significance concerns its symbolic and cultural meanings, that is, the way in which the disease is viewed within society and the expectation the general population has of its sufferers (Bury, 1997).

Most people with long-term illness wish to achieve as good a life as possible within the limits of their symptoms, and actively take steps to ensure this. Here Bury (1991, 1997) distinguishes between 'coping', 'strategy' and 'style'. Coping in this sense does not imply a moral framework used to measure an individual's success or failure in response to their chronic illness, but refers to a more flexible approach to different types of adaptation. This may depend on the nature and severity of the condition, or the extent to which it is discreditable rather than discredited, but it also involves the individual's outlook and sense of self-worth.

Strategies, which lead on from coping, are the mechanisms people adopt in order to live with a changed present and future. Some of these may be actions undertaken by the individual, such as leaving household tasks until the afternoon if pain and stiffness are at their worst on wakening, but others involve social networks or mobilising resources, such as support workers or financial aid. However, the availability of these may be outside the control of individuals.

Different styles of managing chronic illness are bound up with notions of identity and the playing of parts (see Goffman,

1968, chapter 3). Identity is refashioned through the experience of illness, influenced by the individual's level of confidence in the new situation, by social networks and the expected responses from them, and by the availability of resources. Again, though, it should not be seen as a moral imperative for individuals to adapt 'well' and to endure pain 'bravely', even if there is a societal admiration for people who appear, at least to the outside world, to be able to shrug off bodily symptoms. It may be useful here to reread the quotation from Lisa Lynch at the beginning of this chapter for an example of this.

The concept of biographical disruption has been critiqued theoretically, most notably by Simon Williams (2000), who notes firstly that it is premised on a shift from a 'normal' life to a disrupted one, which he describes as an adult-centred model. Someone with a disability or long-term condition from birth or early childhood will incorporate that into their sense of self and normalise it. However, as Larsson and Grassman (2012) demonstrate, disruption can be repeated over the lifespan of people who experience early onset illness, and it cannot always be normalised. Secondly, Williams suggests that illness may actually be anticipated, in particular by those who are older, or from social groups who experience poorer health generally, such as lower socio-economic groups. Illness is just one form of the disruptions that can occur throughout life, such as unemployment, divorce or homelessness, and life experience of adversity may equip people with the skills to deal with such crises. Thirdly, Williams draws on the work of Gareth Williams to argue that rather than chronic illness always causing biographical disruption, biographical disruption may lead to illness, through what he calls 'narrative reconstruction' (Williams, 1984: 175). Two of the three individuals in Gareth Williams' case studies accounted for their ill health (rheumatoid arthritis) as being precipitated by earlier disruptions in their lives, while the third traced her illness back to what can be simplified as 'the will of God'. However, for Betty (the third participant) this had to be situated in the context of other aspects of her life, which she also viewed as part of God's purpose and which had provided her with good fortune. Simon Williams' final criticism concerns the need to consider the timing, context and circumstances within which illness is normalised or problematised. Although these issues are acknowledged in later work (see, for example, Bury, 1997), they are rarely at the centre of the research.

The lasting value of Bury's work lies in its identifying and bringing into sharp focus the consequences of living with long-term conditions in practical situations, and its giving voice to the views of individuals and the strategies undertaken by them. However, as may be expected of a concept that originated over thirty years ago, more recent studies have developed and refined Bury's work, leading to more situational conceptualisations. Indeed, Bury himself has recently commented that biographical disruption may more usefully be viewed as an heuristic device, i.e. an exploratory tool, rather than a concept (Locock and Ziébland, 2015).

Jane Richardson and colleagues conducted a study with eight people with chronic widespread pain, using in-depth serial interviews and diary keeping, the small sample size allowing for intensive data collection (Richardson et al., 2006). They characterised the participants' accounts of the onset of pain using an explanatory framework of 'triggers' (key events) and 'predisposition' (more ambiguous explanations). One participant, Trevor, exemplified a high trigger/high disposition narrative. His account of the onset of his pain includes a period of rheumatic fever which left him with joint and limb weakness, a childhood spent partly in children's homes, and hard manual contract work, all of which in his eyes made him predisposed to illness. The trigger for his widespread pain he describes as follows:

> I was rushing round like somebody gone mad trying to keep up with these young lads, and did the back in while I was working on some valves. This was heavy manual work, I was taken pretty bad with this, . . . and I knew very well what had

happened and gone wrong, . . . but the lad I was working with . . . was a lot younger than me so obviously he was a lot stronger and a lot fitter . . . If I let him down then he would lose his bonus. (Richardson et al., 2006: 1578)

The participants' stories led the researchers to conclude that people with widespread pain can manage their everyday lives, within physical, financial and social limits, although, as can be seen from Trevor's story, things may break down when these limits are exceeded. To that extent biographical disruption and the transformation of self is partial rather than total. In a way similar to Williams' use of narrative reconstruction, the use of trigger and predisposing factors in Richardson et al.'s study gives meaning to experiences, and to lives.

Disruption can thus be seen as a dominant aspect of chronic illness, but this may be nuanced. Both normal and disrupted biographies were seen to co-exist in a sample of twenty-seven people with osteoarthritis and a median age of seventy-six (Sanders et al., 2002). The authors used Bury's distinction between meaning as significance and meaning as consequence, discussed above, as a framework for exploring the impact of symptoms on daily life. Although in common with younger people with chronic illness the participants expe-rienced disruption, the meaning of that disruption differed, and was bound up in their identity as older people, and in their biographical histories. A desire to be seen as independent led to some playing down their symptoms, which, while they were experienced as disruptive, were also viewed as a normal part of ageing.

## Acute pain

Because of the chronic and problematic nature of the expe-rience of pain, the focus of this book is on long-term illness and disability where pain features strongly. Acute pain, on the other hand, tends to be treated as unproblematic due to its transient nature, and the likelihood that it will conform to

Arthur Frank's idea of a restitution narrative. Pain may, however, progress from acute to long term if it does not resolve, and long-term pain may be subject to acute exacerbations, so there are no clear boundaries between these descriptions of pain. Acute pain tends to be the result of trauma, including burns, infection or some therapeutic intervention, although there are exceptions to this. A cause or precipitating factor is more likely to be found for acute than for chronic pain.

The relief of post-operative pain has continued to be a problematic area, despite its poor management having being identified in many surveys over many years. A survey of a random sample of US adults who had undergone surgery within the previous five years assessed the severity of their post-operative pain and their satisfaction with the pain treatments they received (Gan et al., 2014). It found that, despite improving pain relief being a high priority for health policy makers, there has been little improvement in patient satisfaction in analgesia post-surgery. Other research also points to the continuing problem of relieving patients' pain following surgery (Lundborg, 2015).

An example of severe acute pain that may become long term is that experienced following a burns injury. Burns usually occur as an unexpected severe injury, so that a previously healthy person is suddenly plunged into a world of pain and dependency. Pain is a major problem following burns, and studies over many years have continued to report that it is undertreated (Tengvall et al., 2010; Yuxiang et al., 2012). A study from northwest China reported the experience of severe pain in their sample of eight patients, which intensified during the treatment of their wounds. As one participant reported 'Every time when I heard the dressing trolley come, my legs shivered, that pain is truly terrible. I felt like tearing my flesh into pieces or clamping my heart . . . it is splitting, especially during on [sic] my hands dressing' (Yuxiang et al., 2012: 183). Most patients felt that the pain at the time of the burn and the subsequent breakthrough pain were relatively tolerable, but commented on the inadequacy of pain relief during procedures. This finding is consistent with Esfahlan et al. (2010) in their study of pain levels in 100 Iranian patients, which reported mild to moderate background pain, but severe pain during procedures.

In a US study a purposive sample of eight young and middle-aged adults with at least 20 per cent total body surface area burns were interviewed at an average of nine years after the original injury. Persistence of pain, tender scar tissue, sensitivity to temperature and physical limitations were found to be ongoing problems (Abrams et al., 2016). This enduring pain impacted on the ability of the participants to return to normal life; for example, scar tissue on hands affected dexterity, particularly in cold weather. The extent of the burns, however, did not necessarily determine the participants' ability to return to their previous life and employment, with social circumstances and self-efficacy also playing a role.

One reason frequently put forward for the poor relief of acute pain is that health professionals frequently underestimate patients' levels of pain. This issue will be taken up in the following chapter.

## The experience of torture

Torture can be defined as the infliction of pain to destroy, dehumanise and terrorise (Taylor et al., 2013). Amnesty International (2014) reports that methods used include electric shocks, beatings, rape, mock executions, sleep deprivation and long hours spent in contorted positions. In her classic text on pain, Elaine Scarry (1985) defines torture as deliberately inflicting pain in the exercise of power. This exercise of power is seen both in the discourse used to describe torture and by its misdirection, for example by calling it information or intelligence gathering. Scarry draws on numerous sources from literature, art and medicine, as well as testimonies of those who have experienced torture, in order to explore the capacity of one human being to inflict pain on another, and to locate it within power structures as a way of unmaking the world of the victim. She characterises torture in terms of three simultaneous phenomena:

- The infliction of pain. But since 'the infliction of pain on its own would never accomplish the torturer's goal' (Scarry, 1985: 51), this necessitates the following stages.
- The objectification of the subjective attributes of pain. Although the pain itself may be similar to that experienced by others, for example a burn, in the case of torture the pain itself is externalised by virtue of its having been deliberately inflicted by an outside agency.
- The translation of the objectified attributes of pain into the insignia of power. This is made possible through agency (Scarry, 1985: 51). So the weaponry of torture and the power it gives are contingent upon an agent, the torturer. According to Amnesty International, 'Many [governments] are carrying out torture or facilitating it in practice. The political failure by governments is compounded and fuelled by a corrosive state of denial' (2014: 6). Denial allows the torturer to revert back to the first stage, the repeated infliction of torture.

Article 5 of the Universal Declaration of Human Rights of 1948 states that no one should be subjected to torture, or to cruel, inhuman or degrading treatment. With the 1966 International Covenant on Civil and Political Rights, this was enshrined in a legally binding international agreement (Amnesty International, 2014). Despite these agreements, torture still persists in the world today, although the secretive nature of the activity means that the scale of the problem is unknown, and probably under-reported. Between 2009 and 2013 Amnesty received reports of torture and ill-treatment by state officials in 141 countries, across every region of the world. The main reasons for its persistence are the fact that 'governments believe that they benefit from torture, and the persistence of a culture of impunity (the failure to bring to justice those responsible for serious violations of human rights and international humanitarian law)' (Amnesty International, 2014: 12).

Testimonies from the survivors of torture provide a graphic illustration of state involvement in torture (see also Chapter 8), but the secretive nature of imprisonment and torturous acts means that there is rarely independent verification of their experience. The methods of torture and the conditions under which it takes place may mean that a survivor's memory is incomplete and recall distressing (Williams et al., 2010). However, the similarity of reported experience and of the methods used may add to the salience of individual stories, and build up a reliable picture.

An example from Amnesty's reports concerns a sixteen-year-old arrested in Nigeria in 2005 on suspicion of robbery. He stated that police beat him, shot him in the hand and hung him up for hours by his limbs. He said: 'The pain of torture is unbearable. I never thought I would be alive till this day. The pain I went through in the hands of the officers was unimaginable.' In 2013 he was sentenced to death on the basis of a confession signed while being tortured (Amnesty International, 2014: 18). He was pardoned in 2015, but no action was taken against the torturers.

Persistent pain and post-traumatic stress disorder (PTSD) are outcomes of traumatic assault and common among former political prisoners. In this context, however, application of PTSD is limited by its roots in Western biomedicine, and its formulation using non-refugee populations. In their study with nine torture survivors, Taylor et al. (2013), rather than relying on a diagnosis of PTSD, preferred to use the central symptom of re-experience to explore the relationship with persistent pain. All participants had been granted asylum status or indefinite leave to remain in the UK, and were attending a clinic for persistent pain. Participants viewed pain as the enemy, as something inflicted from outside and as separate from the self. It was connected with intrusive memories, either as cause or consequence. For example one respondent reported: 'When they come, the images, the torture, the humiliation, the torture in the prison, you know the whole thing that makes trigger to my pain.' Another said: 'Every day I try to block out the thoughts of what happened to me, suddenly I am walking and then ow! there is this terrible pain in my knee, then it will make me think "Oh, this happened, that happened"' (Taylor et al., 2013: 550). The experience of torture, becoming an asylum seeker, and the persistence of pain constituted multiple losses which changed the identity of the respondents and led to anxiety about the future. More positively, however, they also found help in social support networks and religious faith.

Kolbassia Haoussou informs us that survivors of torture will have specific needs when consulting health professionals. Survivors will often find it hard to trust anyone associated with authority and be suspicious of any questions asked, so clinicians need to explain their role, and the confidential nature of patient–doctor encounters. They should only ask questions about the torture that are absolutely necessary for an understanding of the clinical problem, since flashbacks and nightmares are common. Torture, particularly that including sexual abuse, may also result in shame and stigma, leading to the survivor's reluctance to disclose their experience to others (Haoussou, 2016).

## Summary

The concepts of narrative and of biographical disruption have been, and still are, very influential as frameworks for conducting sociological research into pain, and in healthcare more generally. Many examples of both are to be found throughout this book. Their main strength is that they provide a lens through which to view contextualised and situational personal accounts, accounts that are not usually available to health professionals within the clinical setting.

By its very nature, in-depth qualitative research is carried out with relatively small samples; as such, it is often criticised for being unrepresentative because it focuses on people who are willing to share their story. A counter-argument is that qualitative research recruits individuals who share a common experience, and the building up of many examples of this experience creates a body of knowledge that leads to an understanding of 'what it is like'. There is a considerable consistency to the stories people tell of their experience of pain, and this holds true over many different countries where research has been conducted, and over different cultures. It also needs to be remembered that all research is carried out with people who are willing to participate, and that factor alone may differentiate them from the general population, however large the sample.

Most of the research cited here consists of single interviews, which provide a snapshot of people's lives at a given point in time. But experience is never static, lives and relationships evolve, and a different perspective on pain may have been obtained at another point on the pain trajectory. This does not however detract from the broad findings concerning the difficulties that people in pain face or the complex ways in which they strive to deal with them.

Bury's initial research, like many of the other studies discussed in this chapter, was conducted with people who had been given a reason and a label for their pain. In Chapter 6 we will explore some of the ways in which contested and unexplained pain is viewed and often stigmatised, and the impact this has on the people experiencing it.

CHAPTER FOUR

# Care and Care Services for Pain

It is often difficult to disentangle the experience of pain from the experience of health and social services, and in the context of people's lives there is a close relationship between their pain and the care they receive for it. Some individuals who live with pain may be totally self-managing and self-caring, but for others additional care is required, either temporarily or permanently, for part of the day or continuously. So there is a broad spectrum of need for those in pain.

Traditionally care has been divided into informal (family, friends, community) and formal (paid health professionals). However, this binary division underestimates the expertise and investment of non-professional carers, and overlooks the blurring of caring roles. It also implies a particular type of relationship between those providing care and those receiving it that many people feel does not reflect the reality of their lives. In addition, some who provide physical or emotional support to a close friend or family member do not consider themselves to be 'carers' at all, as they see what they do as part and parcel of the relationship and of a mutual dependency.

In this chapter a number of issues pertinent to the care of someone in pain will be considered, but unlike the previous chapter it will be those carrying out the caring role whose voices will be heard. Provision of services for people in pain and alternatives to conventional care will also be discussed, and the way in which people use, or don't use, the medication prescribed for them.

## Caring for someone in pain

Throughout history the majority of care work has been carried out in the home or in community settings, by people with no formal training. Hospitals are the public face of most developed healthcare systems, but the services they provide are the tip of the healthcare iceberg. Most countries in the West now attempt to relieve pressure on acute services by preventing admission to hospital, and by discharging patients earlier than they did in previous eras. This has led to many more people with long- and short-term illnesses relying on friends and family members to care for them at home. Typically the experience of this group of 'informal carers' has been hidden, their difficulties and the effect on their own lives of their care work taking place behind closed doors. Carers for people with cancer may spend up to 70 hours per week providing personal, social and emotional support and performing practical tasks, and incur an average of £370 in out-of-pocket expenditure during the final three months of the patient's life (Rowland et al., 2017)

Much ethnographic research in this field has been conducted using interviews with individual carers to explore how the caring role impacts on their life and their relationship with the person they care for. When the patient is a child this responsibility falls to the parent(s), who may have little experience of managing pain, apart from during the usual development stages such as teething. For example, when managing postoperative pain in children parents may have concerns about the need to balance their fear of the dangerous side effects of morphine with the need of the child for pain relief (Longard et al., 2016).

Long-term illness and pain frequently occur unexpectedly, following which life becomes increasingly restricted both for the person suffering it and for their carer, who may need to incorporate their new role into their everyday life (see also the discussion of biographical disruption in Chapter 3). Limits are placed on the carer both by the time taken in caring and by the need to be constantly present. The caring role, together with feelings of anxiety and fears about an uncertain future, may have negative implications for the health of the carer (Eriksson and Svedlund, 2006). Their social life may be severely curtailed, leading to feelings of loneliness and isolation, yet many carers still strive to achieve a sense of normality in their lives. Couples may try to maintain a 'normal life' using various strategies, such as keeping their house as a home rather than a sick room, or by restricting visits from professional carers, particularly during the terminal stages of illness. Cohabiting partners may strive to maintain both an individual and a couple identity – a difficult balance that may lead to tensions within the relationship (Aasbø et al., 2016). For example, respondents in a Norwegian study reported that they tried to maintain a 'biographical we' by watching over their dependent partner surreptitiously, and offering care in subtle ways that did not threaten their remaining independence (Aasbø et al., 2016: 790). However, not everyone can achieve this, as illustrated by a female respondent in Eriksson and Svedlund's study: 'There's such sadness in this . . . partly because this change is so noticeable. I mean we have been married to each other since we were in our twenties. And now this change. In the end it feels like "Ah . . . all I am now is a carer"' (2006: 329). The previous intimacy of the relationship had been lost for this woman, leading to a sense of abandonment by her partner.

The caring role may be based on attending to physical needs, but people with long-term pain and their partners may also need emotional and social support. Dyadic interviews (with a couple, interviewed together or separately) can provide an insight into how this is negotiated and played out within relationships. Joint interviews give the opportunity to observe the negotiation, mediation and dominance involved in the production of a joint account, whereas interviewing each partner separately allows them to tell their story from their own perspective, and may make it easier for them to reveal and discuss problematic behaviours (Hudson et al., 2013).

Significant others (spouses, partners or close family members) may play an important role in helping to manage pain and allowing an individual to remain at work. One study (of people with musculoskeletal pain and their partners), which specifically asked participants what helpful or unhelpful things they or their significant other did, found a high degree of congruence between the couples, and a collaborative approach towards the person in pain remaining at work (McCluskey et al., 2015). This appears to be a unique study, as others have focused on more negative behaviours of significant others (see, for example, Waxman et al., 2008). However, this difference may be due to the phrasing of questions, with an explicit focus in the McCluskey study on both positive and negative.

The concept of biographical disruption was used to explore heterosexual couples' experience of living with endometriosis, interviewing the men and women separately and, as far as possible, simultaneously (Culley et al., 2013a; Hudson et al., 2016). This study revealed that actual or anticipated infertility, rather than pain, was often the dominant problem for women with endometriosis, but their male partners did not always appreciate that the impact on fertility was the more pressing issue. Women faced a difficult choice: either accept treatment to relieve the pain, which would delay childbearing; or pursue a pregnancy, and live with severe pain in the meantime. So the couples for which this was an issue had to negotiate, and possibly revise their expectations for the future. Many of the men felt that their partner's views and well-being were paramount, as it was they who were experiencing the symptoms, while at the same time reporting that their own needs were ignored. As one commented: 'The focus clearly has to be on the woman for obvious reasons, she's the one in pain and discomfort . . . but you do at times think "what about me, no one's asked me about how I'm feeling. There are times when you feel that the bloke doesn't get a look-in"' (Culley et al., 2013a: 28).

## The perspective of health professionals on levels of pain

The actions that professional practitioners of any discipline report as undertaking usually conform to the ideal of a professional ethos, rather than their real-world behaviour. Most studies on health professionals' practice are conducted through interviews or self-report surveys in which clinicians tend to report behaviour consistent with professional values. To minimise this limitation a study from Norway on nurses conducting post-operative pain management used both interviews and observation. This dual approach revealed that there were discrepancies between nurses' perceptions of how they dealt with post-operative pain and their actual practice in the clinical setting (Dihle et al., 2006). Although the nurses had good theoretical knowledge of pain assessment and management, this was not always utilised in practice. They relied heavily on their own judgement of patients' pain, or told patients to ring the bell if they required pain relief, both of which strategies led to inadequate pain management. Nurses did not always give the combinations of analgesics that they reported to the researchers as giving, and few gave analgesia during mobilisation of patients. The authors hypothesise that nurses may not always believe the extent of a patient's pain, may be insensitive to the signs of pain, or may believe that patients need to tolerate some degree of pain post-operatively (Dihle et al., 2006). The goal of post-operative pain relief was perceived as being to reduce rather than eradicate pain. Similar results on nurses' knowledge of post-operative pain were obtained from an exploratory study with nurses and patients in the United States. Although all of the nurses acknowledged the patient's judgement of pain as being the most accurate, pain management was inadequate in the surgical units studied (Francis and Fitzpatrick, 2012). Where patients and their assigned nurses were studied together to give a combined nurse/patient perspective, there was still a divergence between patient-reported pain and the levels of analgesia administered by nurses (Watt-Watson et al., 2001).

As nurses are the occupational group who work most consistently with patients in pain, most research has considered their perceptions and management strategies, but other clinicians can also influence the prescribing and administering of analgesia. A questionnaire survey from Italy on the knowledge of doctors and nurses about pain found that there were knowledge deficits and erroneous beliefs in both groups that could lead to inadequate pain relief (Visentin et al., 2001). Health professional's attitudes towards and beliefs about patients in pain are explored further in Chapter 8.

## Pain rating scales

Pain rating scales (PRSs) are a common way for health professionals to assess levels of pain in patients, and to make judgements about the required amount of analgesia. They are also used to assess the effectiveness of treatment by comparing patients' scores at different time periods. The most commonly used is the McGill Pain Questionnaire (MPQ), which uses descriptors of pain to formulate a pain score, but other numeric or visual analogue scales are also widely used. There are also disease- or condition-specific scales such as the Oxford hip and knee score. Within healthcare, pain rating scales tend to be taken for granted as objective measures of pain levels, and treated unproblematically (Denny, 2009a). However, by scoring pain using quantitative measures, rating scales may fail to capture the intensity and experience of pain. Research on the different tools in use has tended to focus on measuring validity and reliability, and the voice of those using them has largely been missing (Williams et al., 2000; Robinson-Papp et al., 2015). People living with long-term pain will often experience different types of pain and may choose to emphasise one over the others when completing the PRS. A study in London with seventy-eight patients undergoing a pain-management programme found that participants incorporated multiple dimensions into their scores, with a particular emphasis on mobility and functioning. There was also a lack of concordance and consistency within and between patients, with some aggregating various pains while others reported one particular pain (Williams et al., 2000). In a focus group study with thirty-six people experiencing low back pain or neuropathic pain due to HIV or diabetes, the participants identified a number of issues with using the pain scales (Robinson-Papp et al., 2015). Common among all groups was the complaint that it was impossible to measure pain in a meaningful way, as they were attempting to quantify a subjective experience influenced by situational factors. The group experiencing neuropathic pain also had problems defining what constitutes pain. For example, many people were bothered by numbness or tingling which could keep them awake at night, but some questioned whether this could actually be described as pain. Other problematic issues raised included averaging pain, as required by some scales, and a tendency to avoid the extremes of the scales (Robinson-Papp et al., 2015).

While PRSs may be used to compare levels of pain at different stages of a long-term illness, they are also used for short periods to assess post-operative pain and the effectiveness of analgesia. Using them for this purpose seems to be less problematic, with patients commenting that the 'common language' of the PRS facilitates dialogue between them and the health professionals (Eriksson et al., 2014: 44). However, these patients also commented on the inability of a PRS to fully describe their pain, and felt that health professionals also had a responsibility to be sensitive to the signs of pain. What these qualitative studies show is that the use of PRSs is not unproblematic, and the definition and rating of pain is a complex and multifactorial task. This issue is taken up again in Chapter 8.

Crawford (2009) has used the example of phantom-limb pain to demonstrate how a specific language around pain emerged and crystallised with the development of the McGill

Pain Questionnaire. She notes that many scholars have argued that because the experience of pain is intensely private (see, for example, Baszanger, 1992), no one can really know another's pain as we lack a language to truly describe it. As Scarry writes, 'physical pain does not merely resist language but actively destroys it' (1985: 4), leading to sounds and cries of pain similar to the sounds humans make before they learn to speak. However, Crawford counter-argues that, rather than being private and unsharable, facets of pain are constituted in and through a shared discourse, which has coincided with the emergence of pain medicine as a discipline over the second half of the twentieth century (see the section on pain clinics, below). The case of phantom-limb pain illustrates how shifts in language became embedded in medical discourse and effectively accentuated pain. Before the middle of the twentieth century, missing limbs were given various names, such as 'ghostly member' and 'limbs invisible' (Crawford, 2009: 656), and associated with sensations like tickling, itching, numbness and pressure as well as pain. During the inter-war years, these phantom limb sensations (which were also experienced in other missing parts of the body) were viewed as the result of denial that the limb was gone, and often described as hallucinatory and pleasurable. The shift to phantom-limb pain, along with its increasing incidence, correlated with theorising around pain, pain medicine and the development of the MPQ by Ronald Melsack (see also the section on gate-control theory in Chapter 1 above). Crawford reports some confusion over whether the descriptors for the MPQ were patient- or literature-generated, which seems to derive from questions over whether medical literature or patient narratives were given greater credibility at any one point in time. However, the MPQ did establish a set of descriptors which helped to provide a common language and capture the qualitative dimensions of pain. Scarry points out that this was achieved not through the invention of new descriptive words but by uncovering 'a structure residing in the narrow, already existing vocabulary originated by patients themselves' (1985: 8). Crawford describes its advent as 'a pivotal moment in the maturation of pain medicine' (2009: 658) and a means by which pain was institutionalised. Returning to the example of phantom limb, following the invention of pain medicine it became codified as painful, while all other previous descriptions disappeared. This was facilitated by the terminology of the MPQ, which became the mode of expressing and understanding the nature of phantom sensation (Crawford, 2009).

In summary, although PRSs are a useful tool in the armoury of pain assessment they need to be used purely as a numeric description of pain, but with account taken of individual factors and context.

## Pain during procedures

In the previous chapter it was noted that the pain experienced during clinical procedures may be more traumatic than the medical problem itself. This is particularly the case for children in pain. Video observation of parents communicating with children undergoing painful treatments for cancer was analysed to produce a typology of four patterns of communication (Cline et al., 2006). In the first pattern, parents normalised the procedure and incorporated it into everyday activities, using games or talk about non-medical topics, thereby distracting the child from what was happening to them. In the second pattern, invalidating parents denied the child's experience, or sought to minimise its validity. Here the parent's role was judgemental. In the third pattern, parents engaged in supportive, empathetic responses to the child, both verbally and non-verbally, acting as comforter and protector. In the fourth pattern, parents distanced themselves, physically or emotionally, and although they may have communicated with others, they were disengaged and distant with the child. Normalising and supporting are categorised as relational strategies: parents and child are together in the painful situation (supportive), or collude in creating an illusion of the medical event being part of normal life (normalising). By contrast, parents using a distancing pattern are avoiding the demands of the situation, the implication being that the child must cope alone. An invalidating communication pattern denies the distressing situation, and invalidates the child's reaction to it (Cline et al., 2006).

Parents with children in hospital often feel passive, reporting that they have limited involvement in their child's care, although nurses may feel that parents do provide care. They are reluctant to complain about their lack of involvement in their child's pain relief, as they do not want to appear 'pushy', or to become unpopular with the nurses (Simons et al., 2001). The idea of people holding back from saying what they want to say, or wanting to create the right impression with health professionals, is a recurring theme in the literature on pain, particularly that on long-term conditions, and it will be raised again in regard to contested illness. What is meant by 'involvement' is subject to interpretation, and may range from being present to taking the initiative in a situation, from helping out to negotiated decision making. So parents and healthcare staff may have different expectations about parental involvement in a child's care. Simons et al. (2001) suggest that healthcare staff will always retain control over a patient's care and may be reluctant to relinquish any part of this; they may also anticipate an increase in demands, and therefore extra work, from parents who take a more active role.

Nurses have been found to under-assess and under-treat pain, with some research suggesting that the more experienced the nurse, the more likely they are to be less sensitive to an individual's pain and their need for pain relief (Nagy, 1999). Chapter 3 discussed the distress felt by patients with severe burns during painful procedures, but healthcare staff also find the nursing of patients with burns a difficult challenge, with many reporting feelings of powerlessness in the management of severe burns (Martins et al., 2014). Nagy (1999) reports various strategies used by nurses in order to carry out procedures,

which include the seemingly dichotomous positions of distancing from or engaging with the patient. A small group of
nurses in Nagy's study attempted to reconcile their caring role
with the need to inflict pain, but whichever strategy nurses
adopted the rationale was always to act in the best interests of
the patient.

## Pain clinics

As mentioned in Chapter 1, pain first emerged as a specialist area of medicine in the 1950s; prior to this it was treated
as a symptom of an underlying cause, and this cause tended
to define it. The shift to pain being constructed as an independent entity, requiring treatment for itself, followed the
increasing visibility of long-term pain within formal healthcare systems (Baszanger, 1989). This required a move from
the laboratory (where causal links are made) to the clinic, a
wider range of professionals to treat pain within specialist
clinics (what became known as the multi-disciplinary team),
and the creation of a 'world of pain' which fragmented into
sub-specialisms for cancer pain, chronic pain, neuropathic
pain, etc. (Clark, 1999: 728; see also Baszanger, 1998). As a
consequence, biomedical theories of pain and the mind/body
dualism began to be opened up to challenge. This was particularly true in the case of chronic or long-term pain for which,
unlike much acute pain or labour pain, no definitive explanation could be found. This move coincided with increasing
expectations of healthcare, with some notable improvements
in treatment fuelling ideas of what medicine could achieve
(James and Field, 1992).

   Although most people continue to be treated for pain by
a clinician treating an underlying condition, there has been
an increase in the number of specialist pain clinics, where
the primary focus is on managing and/or relieving pain for
those whose pain seems intractable despite treatment, and
for those whose pain remains unexplained (see Chapter 6).

Most research on pain clinics focuses on patient satisfaction, using questionnaires in the clinic setting (Trentman et al., 2014; Calpin et al., 2016). Calpin et al. surveyed patients with chronic pain and their clinicians about their expectations of a pain clinic, and found some concordance between them, but also some areas of difference. The expectations of the patients focused on pain relief, education on the cause of the pain, and a diagnosis, whereas the most important issue for clinicians was the formulation and communication of a management plan. Although pain relief would satisfy both patients and doctors, any lack of improvement in levels of pain would cause greatest dissatisfaction for patients, whereas causing more harm than good would disappoint doctors most.

Studies that have used a qualitative approach to explore pain clinics include those of Bendelow and Williams (1996) in the UK, Vrancken (1989) in the Netherlands and Baszanger (1992, 1998) in France. In the British study the pain clinic was seen as a 'dumping ground' for those people whose pain was complex and chronic, and who were viewed by staff as low-status patients. However, younger patients both spent a shorter time in pain and were referred earlier to the clinic (Bendelow and Williams, 1996: 1130). From interviewing patients, the study found that they fell into two broad groups: those who were resigned to the pain, and felt that it dominated their lives, and a much smaller group who accommodated it in their lives, and developed mechanisms to help them cope. The resignation group were both more dependent on the clinical techniques used in the clinic and more critical of them. The accommodation group were independent and highly motivated, and were as a result more acceptable to the staff. This group was more likely to be positive about the clinic and satisfied with their treatment. Patient numbers in the clinic showed a big gender difference, and staff expressed the view that this was because women were more likely to perceive themselves to be in pain, particularly if it was psychological in origin, and more likely to give in to it. This was not borne out by the data, however, as 50 per cent of women but only 25 per cent of men belonged to the accommodation group (gender difference in pain experience is taken up again in Chapter 5).

In the Dutch study, Vrancken (1989) interviewed physicians and psychologists at eight pain centres, and an anaesthetist at a pain block clinic. She identified five approaches to the treatment of pain among the participants, on a continuum from the highly medicalised model or somato-technical approach, to the consciousness approach where pain is viewed as an aspect of being human, and pain experience brings into sharp relief the part of the body where pain is felt. Treatments offered in centres taking a somato-technical approach tended to be medical, focusing on the blocking or easing of pain using opiates or surgery, whereas there were no specific treatments for the consciousness approach, the aim being to establish a relationship with the patient, helping them to either manage the pain, or supporting them until the pain disappeared.

Similarly, Isobelle Baszanger noted that the two pain centres observed in her study conformed to two poles. These she termed 'curing through techniques', based on a biomedical model, and 'healing through adaptation', where pain was defined as poorly adapted behaviour (Baszanger, 1992: 182). In the former the aim was to cure pain through drugs, physical therapies and surgery, whereas in the latter approach the goal of treatment was to control it using a holistic approach, which included cognitive and behavioural techniques as well as drugs and physical therapy.

What these studies demonstrate is that there is no definitive treatment for chronic and long-term pain, and that approaches vary within healthcare systems and according to the beliefs of the clinicians providing care. As Baszanger (1992) argues, interventions are organised around the operational knowledge and practical arrangements of theoretical facts by physicians. The boundaries of medical knowledge are so broad as to accommodate widely differing approaches to care, particularly for conditions such as chronic pain on which there is no consensus view, and where a range of clinicians is involved from a variety of professional and theoretical positions.

## The hospice movement

Typically patients at pain clinics are living with their pain, but a specialism developed from the 1960s aimed to improve management of the pain of the dying. Cicely Saunders (1918–2005) is seen as the founder not only of the first modern hospice (St Christopher's in London), but also of a worldwide movement that advocated a new approach to the care of the dying (Clark, 1999). Saunders had worked at St Joseph's Hospice, where most patients were referred for management of the final stages of cancer, and her communication with the patients there was influenced by her background as a nurse, social worker, doctor and politics graduate. Later these experiences informed her ideas on the concept of 'total pain'. Her interviews with patients revealed that their pain had not been well controlled, and many had been admitted to the hospice only after months of severe pain. While conducting her research, she found that the usual method of medical research, the clinical trial, was not appropriate to researching pain, so instead she compiled detailed descriptive records of the patients' pain and its management. She was 'concerned not only to *understand* the world of pain, but also to *change* it' (Clark, 1999: 730, emphasis in original). The ethos of the hospice movement was to anticipate pain and to alleviate it, rather than wait until the pain was severe before administering analgesia.

Interestingly, Clark identifies a paradox here, as the constant control of pain by clinicians extends to the control of patients who are no longer required to request medication when they need it, but instead have their needs assessed and responded to by others. However, it is in the recognition and management of the wider aspects of pain that Saunders' work was ground-breaking. Influenced by her evangelical Christian beliefs, she saw that mental distress could be more intractable than physical pain, and should also be taken into account in work with the terminally ill. She was also critical of the then current practice of informing a patient's relatives of a terminal diagnosis, but not the patient, a burden which could cause guilt and self-reproach; she preferred an individualised approach to information giving. Although Saunders' early idea of total pain emerged from everyday practice, it eventually became theorised as a concept encapsulating physical symptoms and psychological, social and emotional problems. To this extent total pain can be viewed as 'slightly imperialist', 'an elaboration of the clinical gaze, a new mode of surveillance and an extension of medical dominion' (Clark, 1999: 734; see also Chapter 2 above). James and Field describe the move towards hospice care as a 'charismatic movement' which could only succeed as it resonated with tensions within the broader social context, in particular the provision of poor care and pain relief for the dying (1992: 1363).

Four key elements of charisma can be observed in the development of the hospice movement. First, a highly visible leader with, second, a spiritual calling that attracted many followers; third, a narrow focus on hospice care for the dying; finally, the movement's unique, oppositional model of care. The hospice movement had to be located outside of the NHS, with its traditional methods of treatment, in order to provide a different way of managing pain. However, hospices increasingly became incorporated into mainstream care, at least in part, for a number of reasons. A requirement of a charismatic movement is the existence of 'disciples' to continue the work, but their motivation and intentions are unpredictable and may have unforeseen consequences. In this case, the appropriation of terminal care into a new medical sub-specialism, palliative medicine, gave primacy to medical treatments. Having become a large movement, the routinisation necessary to manage the increasing numbers of hospices and range of services inevitably led to bureaucratisation in terms of hierarchical structures of authority, accountability, and the need

for training and career paths. Nevertheless, the hospice movement did transform the way the care of the dying was managed
in terms of delivering pain relief, honesty in communication,
and emotional support, and it continues to give this care,
despite having been reintegrated with the mainstream health
service, at least in the UK (James and Field, 1992).

Expertise in symptom control, in particular pain relief, and
emotional support ('someone to talk to') are the main expectations of a specialist palliative care service, although some
patients and their relatives have the misconception that it will
provide hands-on care as well (Jarrett et al., 1999). This may be
due to commonly held ideas of what doctors and nurses 'do'.
Some also have the expectation of receiving purely psychosocial
support and symptom control, which is the traditional, more
restrictive role of hospice care in the terminal phase of disease.
Modern services are provided from before to beyond the terminal stages of illness. Palliative care is still, however, associated
primarily with cancer care, and perhaps HIV, meaning that
individuals with other diseases, such as heart failure, which
tends to produce a similar symptom-burden and prognosis,
receive palliative care less often. Healthcare providers in one
American study used the terms 'hospice' and 'palliative care'
interchangeably, and viewed both as forms of terminal care,
which they did not see as appropriate for the long-term care of
heart failure (Kavalieratos et al., 2014). Barriers to palliative
care have thus included confusion about the term itself, the
unpredictability of heart failure trajectories, and the demarca-
tion between curing and caring models of care.

## Alternative and complementary therapy

The terms 'alternative' and 'complementary' therapy are often
used interchangeably or together (complementary and alternative medicine, CAM). The difference between them concerns
whether the therapies are adopted instead of or in addition
to formal health services, since the therapies themselves

– acupuncture, meditation, aromatherapy or massage, for example – are the same. By framing the issue in these terms ('alternative' and 'complementary'), such therapies are constructed in relation to conventional medicine, which reinforces the hegemony of biomedicine within society. There is a debate about whether one word is more appropriate than the other, Mike Saks (1998) commenting that 'alternative therapy' better describes a range of practices that do not receive support from the medical establishment (in the UK context), whereas Ursula Sharma (1996) argues that 'complementary' therapy is preferable as it implies a cooperation with biomedicine. There is also no real consensus over which treatments are to be included under these rather vague terms, which encompass such widely different therapies such as osteopathy and aromatherapy.

There is little evidence for the clinical or cost effectiveness of CAMs from clinical trials, but this criticism can also be laid at the door of many conventional treatments. Randomised clinical trials, particularly those placebo controlled, are unsuitable for assessing many CAMs, and it is unlikely that any one research method will provide a robust evidence base for their use (Black and Rowling, 2009). This lack of evidence has meant that CAMs remain outside of, or marginal to, mainstream medical practice in many healthcare systems.

Individuals may turn to CAMs because of dissatisfaction with previous biomedical treatment or because the treatment offered is not acceptable to them. In their study with women with endometriosis, Marcovic et al. report participants rejecting a biomedical approach and seeking alternatives as 'narratives of contest' (2008: 361), their disillusionment with the treatments offered leading them to seek other remedies. Women can feel empowered by rejecting the biomedical approach, allowing them to take control of their lives (Cox et al., 2003; Marcovic et al., 2008). However, some women with pelvic pain will disengage with medical services in a less positive way, drifting in and out of formal healthcare because they feel disempowered and invalidated (McGowan et al., 2007).

While disengaged, they may use alternative therapies in an attempt to alleviate pain.

Participants in Sharma's research with people who had used therapies outside of a biomedical framework reported a variety of reasons for their decision, not all of which were concerned with how effective they found conventional treatment. Some people were unwilling to risk side effects of treatments, or had not wanted to undergo surgery, while at the same time accepting that these would have ameliorated their present-ing problem. Others, described by Sharma as 'eclectic users' (1996: 239), made what they considered the most appropriate decision in a given situation in relation to each system. Nurses tend to view conventional medicine as the default option, but also perceive complementary therapies as offsetting its limi-tations, and as empowering patients. However, a systematic review of nurses who offered complementary therapies in their work also identified scepticism amongst colleagues and institutional cultures as barriers to their use in hospital set-tings (Hall et al., 2017).

Most research finds that people tend to use conventional medicine before turning to or adding on CAMs (Sharma, 1996; Cox et al., 2003; Marcovic et al., 2008). A longitudinal study that looked at how the expectations of participants using CAMs for low back pain changed over time found that initial vague hopes of treatments were later replaced by expectations around lifestyle and 'whole person connections' (Eaves et al., 2015: 4). Follow-up interviews suggested that participants took a more embodied approach to their pain, and to life generally, as time went on. These shifts could be explained by people seek-ing CAMs (and in particular the types of CAMs in the study: yoga, acupuncture, massage and chiropractic) being more engaged with their own care, or conversely by participation in these therapies leading to increased motivation. Changes in patient expectations may also have been influenced by the ethos of CAM practitioners, who do not see themselves as pro-viding a 'fix' for presenting problems, in accordance with a biomedical approach, but rather as educating individuals in their own role in the healing process, in terms of lifestyle and self-responsibility (Schafer et al., 2012).

## Adherence to medical advice

One area of pain medication that has received critical attention of late is adherence, or how and whether individuals follow the advice given by health professionals. Before considering this issue it is useful to begin by thinking about current terminology, and how it is utilised to construct a particular discourse around medical treatments.

The original term used, particularly in medical literature, was 'compliance', referring to the extent to which a patient followed a prescription or advice from a health professional. This reflected the paternalistic nature of healthcare. The onus was on the patient to follow passively the instructions given. The term commonly used at present, 'adherence', implies some degree of user agreement with what a health professional advises, but often the terms 'compliance' and 'adherence' are used interchangeably and there is much ambiguity surrounding their definitions (Bissonette, 2008). In an early paper, Donovan and Blake (1992) argue that the concept of compliance is irrelevant to most patients, who will weigh up the costs and risks of treatments against the perceived benefits, and make decisions based on this. More recently the non-hierarchical term 'concordance' has been suggested as reflecting a more egalitarian professional-patient relationship, but as yet its use is minimal, possibly because it has also been described as 'concealed coercion' (Pound et al., 2005).

The whole notion of compliance/adherence/concordance is constructed within a biomedical framework, and most research in this area has focused upon increasing the extent to which people follow medical advice, particularly those from stigmatised and vulnerable groups in society. In medical journals the focus of debate has been around how to identify and quantify individuals who do not conform, which locates the problem within patients (Britten, 2001; Sabaté, 2003), who are often labelled as irrational or deviant (Russell et al., 2003).

Individuals' decision-making processes are complex, and they will make use of medication and other therapies in a way that makes sense within the context of their lives. Many personal and structural factors will influence their ability to make choices, yet they often feel that they are viewed as irrational or deviant by health professionals if their choices are not consistent with advice (Playle and Keeley, 1998). Ersek et al. (1999), for example, found that barriers to taking opioid analgesia among patients with cancer were rooted in past and present experience, and in expectations of the future (see also Margaret's story in the section on Illness Narratives, Chapter 3). In their study of rheumatology patients, Donovan and Blake (1992) found different levels of divergence from prescriptions, for example taking higher doses of painkillers when needed rather than equally spaced doses, or taking medication prescribed for someone else that was found to be effective. Most people who did not take medication as prescribed took lower doses, because they feared side effects and wished to take as small a dose as possible. These authors suggest that the implications of compliance are exacerbated when the place from which a drug or other prescription is issued is spatially distant from where it is to be used. This is illustrated by the fact that the highest level of divergence between prescription and use occurred among the twenty-three patients who were given braces or resting splints to relieve pain, only four of whom used them. The others found that they aggravated pain in other joints, or were ugly or cumbersome. So, far from being irrational or deviant, these patients followed the medical advice only when it made sense within their lives.

Similarly, Pound et al. (2005), in a synthesis of qualitative studies on long-term illness, found that most people would try medication and evaluate it in terms of costs and benefits in relation to side effects and the impact on their lives. One of the key reasons why medicines are not taken is concern about the drugs themselves, yet these concerns have tended to be marginalised within the healthcare system. For example, a patient with head and neck cancer explained her dilemma with taking an analgesic which then caused other symptoms: 'It's like if you use that medication, then you have to take the other for the stomach . . . and if you take that one . . .' (Schaller et al., 2015: 339). Health professionals don't always recognise that patients do not always view drug regimes, especially for medications taken over a long period, as prescriptions to be followed rigidly, but as a resource to be used as they see fit. Doses of medication are formulated for the average person, and while this may work at a population level, at a personal level they will not always have the effects intended.

## Summary

The majority of caring work is carried out not within hospitals and clinics, but within the home and community, with many carers providing complex care over long periods, sometimes unaided, and often to the detriment of their own health in the process. Some of these individuals do not consider themselves carers at all, as what they do is part of their partnership or parenting role, an expectation of their relationship.

This chapter has demonstrated the diversity of professional services available for pain. For people with long-term pain these are not always perceived as meeting their specific needs, and they may shop around, as one service or treatment is found not to be of benefit. Patient dissatisfaction may also result from a dissonance between patients and health professionals about the goal of services and treatments, and what they can achieve.

The existence of multiple providers, and people's willingness to access them, may be a reflection of dissatisfaction with mainstream services, but it may also indicate a shift in the way people think about and access pain services. It is possible that patients are becoming less amenable to paternalistic professional advice and more willing to question, and to choose to make treatment decisions for themselves. Exercising choice may involve disengaging from conventional medicine altogether and searching for alternatives. Some will be empowered by this, but for others it is a sign of desperation in the face of continual pain. As people increasingly question health professionals and refuse to passively accept what they are prescribed, clinicians need to rethink how patients make sense of and use prescription and other medicines and therapies. What seems appropriate when discussed in the clinic may turn out to be very different when the drug or appliance is used in the home.

There are, however, success stories, as the development of the hospice movement demonstrates. Once very poorly treated, pain in the terminally ill has become a specialist service, although in the process the hospice movement ethos has had to adapt to fit into the dominant healthcare model and funding mechanisms.

# CHAPTER FIVE

# Structures of Diversity and Pain

It is a self-evident truth to say that societies are diverse. Age, ethnicity, gender, economic status and dis/ability all vary to a greater or lesser extent between and within societies. In this chapter some of these concepts will be considered in relation to the experience of pain. Although for clarity they will be addressed separately, it is important to note that we are all categorised, or categorise ourselves, in different ways in different situations, and, as was noted in Chapter 2, we all play many parts. We need to avoid the risk of essentialising any one social categorisation above another, as each is contextual. It is also important not to treat social categories as fixed or bounded, since time, events and social awareness may cause them to change at both society and individual level. Social groups are heterogeneous, so in discussing, for example, gender we need to be aware that the experiences and expectations in life of a professional white woman will be qualitatively different from those of a disabled black woman, so that a discussion about women cannot assume homogeneity. Each structural factor is one variable which intersects dynamically with others to capture, at a given moment in time, a complete picture. So, for example, a study that considers pain relief in black children (Goyal et al., 2015) appears in this chapter in the section on race and ethnicity, as that was the focus of the research. But since age is also a relevant variable, it could equally have been placed in the section on children and pain.

## Gender

When we talk about gender we are delineating social group-ings and the attributes typically associated with being male or female. Individuals, however, will conform to a varying degree to these attributes, and the growing awareness of people who identify as homosexual, bisexual, transgender, intersex and pangender means that traditional binary divisions of how people view themselves and how others perceive them are becoming more problematic.

Very little research on pain adopted gender as a key variable before the ground-breaking work of Gillian Bendelow. Her development of a sociology of pain and gender has provided the conceptual basis for much of the work that has followed since. Central to her thinking is that 'the dominance of a somatic ideol-ogy inherent in medicine tends to define emotional expression in experiences of pain as socially undesirable, whereas suppres-sion through mechanisms such as stoicism tends to be highly valued' (Bendelow, 2000: 40; see also the section on 'culture' in this chapter, and Chapter 7). This moral evaluation, Bendelow hypothesises, may be gendered. The fieldwork for her research took place in a GP surgery, and utilised a mixed-methods approach. A questionnaire examining beliefs about health, ill-ness and pain was given to 121 men and women, followed by more in-depth interviews with a sub-sample of twenty-one exploring the complexities of attitudes and beliefs about pain. The two major findings of the questionnaire were that:

1. Most people believed either that women possess a greater capacity for coping with pain or that there are no gender differences. Only a minority thought that men coped better with pain. When asked why this was so, women's reproduc-tive role was frequently cited.
2. Men were significantly less inclined than women to think that the emotional component of pain perception was important. (Bendelow, 2000: 90)

More elaborate responses that help to explain these find-ings were obtained from the interviews. The belief in women's greater pain capacity is at variance with experimental psycho-logical research that tends to show women as possessing lower pain thresholds than men. Participants explained this in terms of women being more attuned to pain in their everyday lives from puberty onwards because of their reproductive function. These views are consistent with the process of socialisation whereby men are expected to be stoical when in pain, and are discouraged from expressing pain. Men will incorporate these expectations into dealing with serious illness, such as cancer. While advice from health professionals on the clinical aspects of care may be accepted uncritically, men may avoid asking for help and find it difficult to engage emotional support (Wenger and Oliffe, 2014). Women on the other hand are seen as more likely to report pain, and to act on symptoms without feeling threatened by admitting to vulnerability. So the experience of pain among Bendelow's respondents was seen as 'natural' for women, but 'abnormal' for men (Bendelow and Williams, 2002). A complex web of biological and sociocultural explana-tions for gender differences in pain perception can be observed in the responses in this research.

The existence of emotional or psychological pain was acknowledged by both sexes, but there was a belief that a level of stigma was associated with revealing such pain. This idea will be explored in more detail in Chapter 7, but since here we are concerned with gender differences in perceptions, the important point to note is that men more than women thought this to be the case. Women were more likely to provide holistic overviews of pain. However, physical pain with clear physiological roots was seen by both men and women as more socially acceptable than emotional or psychological pain, lead-ing to a belief in a hierarchy of pain (hierarchical approaches to pain by health professionals will be discussed in Chapter 8).

Following on from Bendelow's work, a number of research projects on pain and gender have been conducted, mainly considering gendered health conditions, but also long-term conditions that affect women more than men. A dyadic study on women with endometriosis (see also Chapter 6) reported that some men found it hard to provide support to their partners, while others felt that hiding their own emotions and staying strong and positive was the correct response to their partner's pain. Although women appreciated the support of partners, some would have preferred less stoicism and more understanding (Culley et al., 2013a).

Far less research has been conducted into men's health, but the influence of notions of masculinity on ideas around health is evident in most studies. Men may construct a notion of masculinity using resources available to them that are largely unhealthy. For example, refusing to take time off work when sick, or adopting risky behaviour such as drink-driving, situates them in a masculine arena (Courtenay, 2000). Similarly, experiencing illness can reduce a man's status in masculine hierarchies, and be construed as a sign of weakness. By extension, this reinforcing of masculinity involves a rejection of femininity, with which accessing healthcare and admitting weakness is associated. So a participant in a study on men's health in London reported: 'To get rid of the [headache], I have to eat and sleep, that is my medication. I don't take tablets and I never took a paracetamol in my whole life. I know how to handle myself . . . I am my own GP' (Bogle, undated).

Robertson et al. (2015) have also noted hegemonic discourses of masculinity continuing to be persuasive in relation to mental health. Emotional repression, fear of being seen as weak, and loss of status are all implicated in mental health problems and in suicidal thoughts and actions (see also Chapter 7). Male ego may also be implicated in the unwillingness to seek medical help, although some men do view this as unwise, with the potential to endanger their long-term health (Bogle, undated).

## Gendered pain

More women than men report experiencing long-term pain, and a large number of illnesses characterised by chronic pain have a higher female prevalence (Grace and Zondervan, 2006). In his study on the experience of rheumatoid arthritis discussed in Chapter 3, Bury (1982) interviewed twenty-five women and five men, pointing out that the disease is experienced by four times as many women as men. We must treat such reports with caution, however, as from the discussion above it can be seen that differences in health-seeking behaviour need to be factored in. Men and women have different and complex ways of dealing with pain, which may result in the former being less visible in official numbers and statistics.

Nevertheless, a distinction can be made between painful conditions that are probably experienced more by one sex than the other and conditions that are gendered, that is, in which gender is an integral part of the illness and the experience of it. In Chapter 6, on contested illnesses, the point will be made that conditions are more likely to be contested where they involve a gender bias or where they are gendered conditions, particularly those affecting women. Here we are more concerned with the experience of such conditions, whether contested or not, and, as we will see, the division between contested and non-contested pain may itself be quite blurred, or a false binary.

Many gendered conditions are concerned with problems of women's reproductive health. Problems such as chronic pelvic pain or vulval pain are compounded by the secrecy and revulsion surrounding female genitalia, which is socially conditioned and captured in discourses of pollution and taboo (Seear, 2009; Labuski, 2015). In particular, the labia are absent from discussions about the site of pain, and 'routinely eclipsed – including by gynaecological medicine and so-called sexuality experts – by the vagina and its relationship to coital sex and reproduction' (Labuski, 2015: 235). So painful health problems may remain hidden, with women having to make decisions about disclosure in both the public and the private spheres (Denny, 2004a). Concealment and disclosure cannot be understood without attention to the cultural dimensions of bodily parts (Labuski, 2015), in particular the 'etiquette of menstruation' (Seear, 2009: 1220), in which women are reluctant to openly discuss the subject. Far less is known about the experience of genital pain in men, but it has been suggested that men report it less than women because it is viewed as something 'women get' (Grace and MacBride-Stewart, 2007), and so to do so would threaten their gendered identity (Toye et al., 2014).

Pain during childbirth is possibly the most commonly experienced gendered pain, but unlike other pain it is often viewed as productive, as it is endured for a positive reason and for most women it normally ends with the delivery of a live baby. For some women labour pain will be the worst pain they endure, but for others it will be compared favourably to more chronic and long-term pain. So, for example, women in Bendelow's study reported that labour pain was not the worst they had suffered, and women in a study of sickle cell disease (SCD), discussed below, compared the pain of sickle cell crises unfavourably to the pain of labour (Bendelow and Williams, 2002; Coleman et al., 2016). In Chapter 2 we noted the shift in the construction of labour pain from the 1950s (Arney and Neill, 1982), but Rajan (1996) found that, with the increase in technological help available during childbirth, women do not want to be rendered helpless by drugs and technology, but to give birth with minimal help. The use of TENS and Entonox for pain relief among participants was acceptable as long as they felt themselves to be in control of their use, but since their availability was decided by health professionals and/or organisations, it was the latter who retained ultimate control. In order to circumvent this, women may provide their own TENS machines, suggesting that they are simultaneously both agents in their own care and victims of medicalisation.

## Genital mutilation

Nowhere does gendered pain come into such sharp relief as in the issue of female genital mutilation (FGM), defined as 'all procedures involving partial or total removal of the female genitalia or other injury to the female genital organs whether for cultural or other non-therapeutic reasons' (WHO et al., 1997: 3; for a detailed description of the classification of FGM see Macfarlane and Dorkenoo (2015: 9)). Although the practice is illegal in many parts of the world it is widely carried out on women and girls in some regions, despite it being irreversible and having no therapeutic value. It has no known health benefits and is associated with extreme pain during and after the procedure. Long-term complications include dysmenorrhoea, chronic pain, painful sexual intercourse and complications during labour.

Despite the practice being illegal in Egypt it is still widespread there, especially in rural areas, although it is not unknown among educated urban families. It is carried out on both Muslim and Christian girls. In May 2016 FGM was performed on two sisters in Egypt, following which one girl died (Agence France Presse, 2016). The surgery was performed by a registered doctor in a private hospital. Health professionals are increasingly carrying out FGM on girls in North Africa and the Middle East in countries where the practice is widespread, the rationale being that it is more hygienic and safer than procedures performed by traditional practitioners (see also Chapter 8). This position was espoused in an editorial in *The Economist* in June 2016, where it was argued that as attempts to eradicate the practice have failed, a new approach based on governments banning 'the worst forms' but permitting 'those that cause no lasting harm' should be adopted (Anon, 2016a). The accompanying article points out that in Egypt 61 per cent of girls are cut despite the fact that it is illegal and in defiance of a decade-old religious edict (fatwa) by senior Muslim clerics (Anon, 2016b). In Malaysia FGM is often performed by clinicians as a nick or slit into the clitoral hood on girls between the ages of one and three years, which, it is argued, is less invasive than other forms of cut. Some gynaecologists in the West have also argued that performing a nick or slit into the clitoris or vulva (using the more respectable-sounding term of female genital alteration) does not cause lasting damage, and should be accepted practice in order to prevent more severe types of FGM being carried out (Arora and Jacobs, 2016). These relativist approaches to FGM fail to consider the fact that many rural areas have no access to hygienic medical services. Their proponents also assume the inevitability of a reduction in the practice if it is made illegal through a step-change approach. In the meantime women and girls continue to be subjected to a practice that most of the world views as unnecessary and a violation of an individual's right to bodily integrity and self-determination. Relativism also provides legitimacy to any FGM practice, and by extension to other forms of control over women's bodies, such as breast ironing, which is common in Cameroon, and increasingly among the diaspora. In addition, it reinforces the idea of the female body as tainted, and female sexuality as something to be suppressed.

While not condoning FGM, it is useful to consider why the practice continues in the twenty-first century, and why it is often mothers who have been subjected to it in their own childhood who perpetuate the practice. This may help us to understand the resistance to change and the difficulties that agencies such as UNICEF and the WHO face in working to eradicate it. Like the now-abandoned practice of foot-binding in China, Sati, and dowry and child marriage in many parts of the world, FGM represents the control and subjugation of women and girls, and unequal gender roles (UNAIDS et al., 2008). There is no one set of reasons why FGM is practised, so what follows is a collation of those most commonly cited. All justifications for FGM are bound up with women's position in society, their lack of social and economic power, and their subjection to male domination. In some societies FGM may be part of a coming of age ritual, a necessary step towards adult-hood and acceptance into the community. Women may find themselves outcasts and unmarriageable if they do not have it performed. The clitoris is considered a male organ, and so its removal is necessary to create true femaleness with the associ-ated characteristics of docility and obedience. Men may also demand to marry women who have undergone FGM as proof of virginity and sexual fidelity. In countries where women are given little or no formal education and are not accepted in public without a male escort, their only means of survival is though marriage. When women are economically and politically powerless their choices are constrained by struc-tural determinants. The practice of FGM is a denial of female sexuality, and self-determination, but wider societal changes to the position of women in society are necessary in order to persuade parents and communities to abandon the practice.

It has to be noted that FGM is not prevalent in all societies where women lack power, nor does greater gender equality necessarily result in its cessation. In the first ever compilation of annual statistics for FGM in the UK, 5,700 cases were iden-tified during 2015–16. In eighteen cases the FGM had been undertaken in the UK, including on eleven women and girls who were born in the UK (HSCIC, 2016). The most common age range was between five and nine years. However, in a letter to *The Guardian*, Brenda Kelly (2016), an obstetrician special-ising in FGM, argued that these data, collected at the point of encounter with clinicians, do not provide useful informa-tion on prevalence at a population level. A report from City University, London, used household interview surveys in countries where FGM is practised, the 2011 UK census data, and birth registrations to estimate the prevalence of FGM in the UK. The number of women and girls at risk is increasing due to the increase in migration, with an estimated 137,000 women living in the UK originating from countries where FGM is practised. The report estimated that since 2008 around 1.5 per cent of women giving birth in England and Wales had

had FGM performed (Macfarlane and Dorkenoo, 2015). It is difficult to assess how practices are altered by migration and by living in a society where any collusion in FGM is illegal, so the accuracy of these estimates is limited.

Although FGM is normally considered a gender and human rights issue, male circumcision is not. More than half of all boys in the United States are circumcised, although the number is falling and the practice is far less common in Europe. Some religions have practised male circumcision for centuries, but it became common in the late nineteenth century in the USA as a means of curbing masturbation. Current reasons given include hygiene, appearance and the possibility of teasing by peers if a boy looks different. As with FGM, there is no medical reason for routine circumcision of infants, which is a painful procedure and carries a risk of complications such as infection and the removal of too much skin.

Challenges to the commonly held view that male circum-cision is a minor procedure with long-term benefits are becoming more prevalent, although in many countries, includ-ing the United States, the 'benefit over risk' argument has led to claims that it is unethical not to recommend its use (Morris et al., 2016). Others, mainly from Europe, argue that there are strong financial reasons behind the recommendation of routine male circumcision, as it can be very lucrative for the practitioner, but that it constitutes a human rights violation of the integrity of the body in minors, who lack the ability to give informed consent (Svoboda and van Howe, 2013).

## Race and ethnicity

Ethnicity as a social characteristic is contextual and situational. So, for example, the British history of empire and medicine's justification for the racist treatment of colonised peoples are both relevant for understanding how racial and ethnic differ-ence came to be essentialised and pathologised. In the USA and Australia, being indigenous to the land equates with a socio-economic status worse than that of recently arrived (white) minorities (Ahmad and Bradby, 2007). Minority ethnic status, usually resulting from migration from other countries, is associated with economic, social and health disadvantage. Too often, however, the focus of this disadvantage has been on the 'deficiencies' of minority ethnic cultures rather than on structural factors. An illustration of this can be seen in the prevalence of rickets, a consequence of lack of vitamin D in the diet or from the sun, which causes poor bone development, resulting in bow legs. This was common in the UK in the early twentieth century but was eradicated by the addition of vitamin D to margarine, the introduction of free school milk, and by children having more exposure to the sun. In the 1970s rickets reappeared within South Asian communities in the UK and was redefined as an exotic disease, caused by poor Asian diets and modest clothing. The answer was not to add vitamin D to staple foods as had worked previously, but for Asian communities to adopt Western diets and dress (Ahmad and Bradby, 2007).

Ahmad and Bradby argue that the term 'ethnicity' has become so overly and imprecisely used that it risks losing value as an analytical tool. Despite this limitation, ethnicity is still widely employed in research into pain, with quite diverse definitions of the term. For clarity, and bearing in mind that it is a dynamic concept, ethnicity is understood here as 'characterised by its relationship to forms of heritage (national, linguistic, cultural), notions of belonging and external recognition of such claims, but also by its malleability, flexibility and situationality' (Ahmad and Bradby, 2007: 796). However, as will be seen below, much research uses simplistic and ambivalent divisions such as 'black', 'white' or 'Asian' to denote diversity, with no acknowledgement of ethnic and cultural difference within these groupings. It is often unclear what researchers mean when they use the terms 'race' and 'ethnicity', which they fail to define or operationalise adequately (Lee, 2009).

Many recent studies considering ethnic differences between the levels of pain relief given to black patients and others have been conducted in the United States. While this research is useful to explain disparities in the USA that may be applicable to other countries, the differences in terms of the organisation and funding of health systems, as well as cultural differences, mean that we must be cautious when trying to extrapolate to other settings. Some of this work is retrospective, using data from hospital records, so although it can tell us what happened it does not offer explanations for how ethnicity or race are important factors (Lee, 2009). There are also problems with the accuracy and comparability of record keeping. Other studies are speculative in that they ask people, usually health professionals, how they would behave in a given situation, the 'what if?' question, rather than observe or question what they actually did in practice.

Despite these limitations there is a degree of consistency between the studies in that they all demonstrate ethnicity as a factor in the prescribing of analgesia. Goyal et al. (2015) used hospital records to evaluate racial differences in the administration of analgesia, particularly opioids, among children (defined as under twenty-one years of age) diagnosed with appendicitis. They found in an estimated 940,000 children diagnosed with appendicitis that black patients with moderate pain, as assessed by pain score, were less likely to receive any analgesia, and among those with severe pain black children were less likely to receive opioids than white children. Although this study highlights what may be happening, it does not tell us why; but another US study which conducted research with 100 lay people and 400 medical students and doctors points to one contributing factor (Hoffman et al., 2016). Kelly Hoffman and colleagues offered their participants various true and false statements about racial differences, such as 'black people's nerve endings are less sensitive than white people's' (false) and 'white people are less likely to have a stroke than black people' (true). They also asked participants to

imagine how much pain black and white people would experience in a given situation, and asked the health professionals to
suggest treatment in such situations. They found that among
the lay group those who had most strongly endorsed the false
statements reported lower pain ratings for black people. The
health professionals who endorsed false beliefs also translated
their views into lower pain ratings for black patients and subsequently made less accurate treatment recommendations.
Participants who did not endorse false statements showed no
bias in treatment decisions. The authors conclude that false
beliefs about biological differences between black and white
patients shape the way in which black people are perceived and
treated for pain.

Another US study hypothesised that health professionals
may rely on subjective cues about race/ethnicity and drug
abuse when prescribing opioids for pain-related conditions,
particularly when treating a condition commonly associated
with drug-seeking behaviour, such as back or abdominal pain
(Singhal et al., 2016). Although abuse of prescription opioids
is a growing problem in the USA and elsewhere, inadequately
treated pain is also of concern. Singhal and colleagues tested
this by using freely available hospital data for 2007–11 to review
emergency department visits for non-definitive pain (backache, toothache, abdominal pain) and definitive pain (long
bone fracture, kidney stones) in regards to analgesia prescribed
according to racial/ethnic variables. They found significant
disparities in the prescribing of opioids for non-definitive
pain, particularly in the non-Hispanic black population, even
though death rates from opioid abuse are much higher in the
non-Hispanic white population (Singhal et al., 2016). They
conclude that racial bias influences prescribing behaviour,
and this may be due to stereotypical assumptions made about
substance abuse among various ethnic groups.

A focus on diseases that are found only in certain ethnic
groups reflects racist stereotypes, such as the supposed low
pain threshold and a tendency to analgesia addiction among

African Caribbean people with sickle cell disease (SCD) (Ahmad and Bradby, 2007). In addition, the failure to differentiate between groups and subgroups (for example by defining all peoples from the Indian subcontinent as Asian) means that differences within ethnicities are not captured (Palmer et al., 2007). SCD has a major impact on the life of sufferers, and the actual nature of the pain is poorly understood, so the experience of people with the disease is worth highlighting (Coleman et al., 2016). SCD is associated with severe acute pain during crises, but also with chronic pain due to joint damage and neuropathy. As with many of the diseases highlighted in this book, it impacts on every area of life, including education, employment and social relationships. Sufferers can find the acute pain of SCD so great that they have to resort to extreme analogies to describe it, such as 'someone hammering inside your bone' or 'being set on fire continuously' (Coleman et al., 2016: 196). They also personify the pain and its inescapable nature using war metaphors, such as talking of an ongoing struggle or battle. Participants in a Jamaican study spoke of the disease causing multiple losses – of autonomy, of friends, of career opportunities and of the ability to socialise. They also reported a lack of control during acute episodes, although they also employed strategies to cope, including acceptance of the disease, and attempts to retain control (Anderson and Asnani, 2013).

## Culture

A number of studies in the middle of the twentieth century considered the influence of culture on the experience of symptoms, particularly pain. Cultural assumptions about the significance of symptoms, and ideas about independence or stoicism, are all variables that impact on illness behaviour. In the USA in the 1950s a body of research on different immigrant groups was developed, but some of these studies were limited by the assumptions they made about the homogeneity

of cultural groups, which resulted in stereotypical charac-
terisations. In one study, Italian and Jewish patients were
said to respond emotionally to pain, whereas Old Americans
were said to comply with medical advice and avoid being
difficult (Zola, 1966). Another study found that Irish immi-
grants described their complaints in a matter-of-fact way, as
opposed to Italians who were less specific and more general
(Zborowski, 1952). Despite the methodological difficulties and
the assumptions made about social groups, these studies are
still reported in sociological texts as examples of cultural differences in response to pain.

In his classic work on health, illness and culture, Cecil
Helman (2007) informs us that how people perceive and
respond to pain, and how or whether they communicate it,
are influenced by social and cultural factors. Reponses to pain
may be voluntary or involuntary, and it is the former that are
particularly influenced by such factors. Helman differenti-
ates between 'private' and 'public' pain. Within some cultural
groups it is common to maintain privacy, even when pain is
severe, and this is particularly the case in societies that value
stoicism. This expectation is more pronounced for men than
women, especially young men, and being able to experience
pain without displaying overt signs such as flinching may form
part of initiation rituals marking the transition from boyhood
to manhood. Somali women living in Sweden, for example,
report that Somalis, in particular males, are expected from the
age of about eight to be stoical regarding pain. The capacity to
endure pain is a valued attribute, particularly during acts of
aggression among men (Finnstrom and Soderhamn, 2006).

Whether or not the response to pain moves from being private to public depends on the significance placed on the pain
and whether it is seen as 'normal' or 'abnormal' (the importance of this will be taken up in Chapter 6 when discussing
contested illness). Attitudes to pain are learnt early in life, and
are influenced by family and community. Each social and cultural group will have a unique 'language of distress' (Helman,

2007: 189), a specific way of signalling that a person is in pain. The form this takes depends, among other things, on whether an emotional display of distress is valued. Responses may also change over time as a result of social and technological changes. For example, in 1952 Zborowski wrote that among Polish women labour pains were expected and accepted, whereas in the USA women did not accept pain and demanded analgesia. In the globalised world of the twenty-first century we might expect such differences in expectations to have been reduced or eliminated.

In her study of people's lives and health in the East End of London, Judy Cornwell (1984) also points to the differentiation between public and private accounts of pain. Public accounts were couched in common-sense terms which endeavoured to place the participant in the morally correct position, whether speaking about their own health or someone else's. People were admired for bearing pain cheerfully or for hiding the fact that they were seriously ill. Even those who had quite serious health problems were considered hypochondriacs if they appeared too preoccupied with their health. Participants differentiated between 'normal illness', which could be successfully treated by the medical profession, and 'real illness', which is unusual or severe, and may not be amenable to medical treatments (Cornwell, 1984: 130). Real illnesses were also disabling and possibly life-threatening. Many painful conditions, such as arthritis, rheumatism and abdominal pain, fell into a third category of 'health problems that are not illness' (1984: 131) but part of the natural processes of ageing or reproduction. Public accounts attended to the moral aspects of being ill. Although the illness itself was beyond their control, the approach individuals took to it or the way they coped established moral criteria by which people could be judged 'good' or 'bad'.

Private accounts, on the other hand, were much more concerned with contextualising illness, situating men within the workplace and women as being responsible for the health of the family. Men tended to accept workplace hazards and pains, such as backache, as part of the job. Taking time off sick or putting pressure on employers to introduce better safety measures were not viable options, as either could result in the loss of one's job. However, once at home, men would give into their symptoms and expect their wives to care for them. Women were much less likely to take on this role with their husbands than with their children, to whom they did feel such a responsibility. In terms of their own health, women would try to accommodate any illness into their normal day, and consult a doctor when this was not possible in order to get treatment that would put them back on their feet, and back into their domestic role.

More recently, the notion of acculturation, an important factor ignored in early studies, has been identified as influencing ethnic differences in acute pain sensitivity, with those in the process of getting used to a new cultural environment showing a heightened pain response (Chan et al., 2013). By the second generation pain sensitivity is similar to that of the 'new' country. The mechanism by which this occurs is unclear, but it is possible that the stresses of migration and the fear of discrimination may play a part, and be experienced less in subsequent generations. However, although lower acculturation appears to influence the reporting of pain, it cannot explain all of the differences between new and indigenous populations, and limitations in the definition of 'acculturation' itself may result in assumptions about the extent to which it can account for such difference (Palmer et al., 2007).

## Age

Perspectives on age have mostly been concerned with older people. In particular, the literature on pain has focused on long-term problems that, although not inevitable, are associated with growing older. More recent studies have considered children in pain, but studies of adults excluding the elderly have largely ignored age as a contextual factor, or taken it for granted. Most empirical studies give an age range as part of the description of the participants, but few use it as an analytical category. The King's Fund has argued that the pharmaceutical industry does not take the needs of children and older people fully into account when researching and developing new drugs, rarely recruiting them to trials (Harrison, 2003), which may have serious implications for prescribing medication to these groups.

*Children in pain*
The traditional way in which childhood has been viewed, with children seen as passive and subject to social forces, is giving way to theories of childhood that cast them as social actors (Jenkins, 2015). Childhood is a social construct, a negotiated set of social relationships in early life, and by exploring family interaction using a conversational analysis approach it can be demonstrated that children are active agents in constructing the nature of their experience, including that of pain. Children are capable of producing descriptions of sensations, such as pain, and of claiming the right to accept or deny their parents' reworking of their sensation.

We saw in Chapter 1 that children have been largely ignored historically in writing on pain, or have had their pain viewed as a punishment for sin. Since the 1970s, when Margaret Stacey (1970) first brought to our attention the adverse effects of hospital stays on children, it has been acknowledged that their needs have not been adequately catered for in healthcare settings. It is now recognised that children experience and react to illness and pain in ways that are deserving of special consideration. It is thought that their pain was poorly managed in the past because they could not articulate it as effectively as adults. Other responses to pain, such as withdrawal, were misinterpreted and mismanaged. A study undertaken in the 1940s which concluded that infants and babies were unable to feel pain, since pain sensation required some developmental maturity, was influential in clinical practice up to the 1970s

(Zisk, 2003). Children often underwent surgery with no anaesthesia but only paralysing agents to keep them still during the procedure. Although it is now accepted that children do feel pain, it is still often undertreated, and our understanding of children's expression of pain is poor, particularly in non-specialist settings. There is some confusion about the nature of chronic pain in children, and there are attitudinal barriers to effective care, with the consequent strain placed on families (Maciver et al., 2010).

*Pain in older people*

In Chapter 3 we saw the importance of narratives for communicating pain, and Kleinman (1988) states that illness storytelling is particularly prevalent among the elderly, who will often weave their experience of illness into the seamless plot of their life stories. Older people are also more likely to behave stoically in dealing with pain and to accept it as a normal facet of ageing. Two examples from Sanders et al. demonstrate these assertions:

> I've always done a job that involves a lot of steps and kneeling, and I've always worked because we had this old house that was condemned and you couldn't get new houses during the war, and when my husband came out of the army, we didn't have much money, he was on the buildings so . . . I used to do part-time work . . . Whether it was wear and tear on the knees. But anyway after about 20 years I was walking on two sticks. (2002: 235)

> Well, I don't know but basically you have to face the fact that you're gonna get old and if you get old you have to make adjustments to suit that. (2002: 236)

Those over seventy-five are less likely to receive analgesia and opioids in emergency departments than people aged thirty-five to fifty-four (Platts-Mills et al., 2012). Worry about the possible short- and long-term side effects of opioids in older people explains some of the disparity, but an assessment of the severity of pain is often missing in the records of older people attending emergency departments, suggesting that clinicians are less attentive to pain in older patients. The assessment and management of pain in older people is complex, as many have co-morbidities, concomitant acute and long-term pain, and communication may be difficult due to sensory deficit. For example, an Australian study suggests that nurses in an elderly assessment unit communicate more with each other when assessing a patient's pain, and will only ask the patient simplistic questions, which could lead to ambiguities in interpreting their level of pain (Manias, 2012).

Older people are also less likely to be involved in research on cancer and cancer pain, even though the incidence of most cancers increases with age (Dunham et al., 2013). A review of the literature on cancer pain and older people found that they equated pain, particularly increasing pain, with disease progression, and that this provoked anxiety about death and dying. Fear of pain was also bound up with fears about the side effects of analgesics (Dunham et al., 2013). These issues may also be relevant to younger people, but the absence of research on older people, including the exclusion of over-sixty-fives from research samples, means that the unique needs of this population have not been adequately addressed.

## Disability

Although much of this book is concerned with how pain is associated with disability, little attention has been paid thus far to the way in which disabled people are treated when they are in pain. Children with profound special needs face particular challenges in receiving adequate pain relief. Pain is common among this group of children, and yet assessment frequently relies on the child's behaviour and informal reports from families (Carter et al., 2002). This is compounded by a commonly held but erroneous belief that people with learning disabilities (LD) have a higher pain threshold than the general population (Findlay et al., 2014). Parents in Carter's study described pain of spasticity, gastro-intestinal pain, pain related to handling or moving, and sore ears (being problematic pressure points), all of which they managed by a mixture of guesswork about the cause of pain, working out what to do to relieve it, or acting intuitively, the last two coming from their experience of caring for the child (Carter et al., 2002).

Emily Smith, a person with Down's syndrome who is an expert by experience at Nottingham University, reports that people with LD are often not listened to when they report pain, and not treated by health professionals in the same way as someone without a cognitive impairment would be (Smith, 2016). There is of course a wide variation in the ability to articulate pain, but people with LD tend to locate pain on the upper end of rating scales. This may be because those with a reduced cognitive capacity have fewer coping skills, and therefore experience pain more severely, or because their previous experience of not being believed may encourage them to describe the pain as severe (Findlay et al., 2014). Whatever the reason, the result is that adequate pain management is not always delivered to people with cognitive disability.

## Summary

This chapter has considered how structures of diversity may impact on the experience of pain and on the treatments received. Preconceptions held by health professionals and the wider population about individuals due to their social characteristics may result in them being misunderstood or treated with suspicion, which may have serious consequences for their care.

In discussing social structures there are certain pitfalls that need to be avoided. The first – essentialising areas of diversity, such as gender or ethnicity – was highlighted in the introduction. To reiterate, each individual is a complex mix of characteristics, and at any one time different structural factors will assume importance in their lives. Structures of diversity intersect, and are contextual and situational. The second, and related, issue is the question of agency: who is speaking for whom? In interpreting research findings it is easy to assume that voices and narratives are representative of a social group, but that cannot be taken for granted. Examining recruitment methods may reveal that participants are from a specific sub-group. It is also frequently the case that research samples have a lot in common with the wider population, who do not suffer from the condition under investigation (see also Chapter 6). The third pitfall is the tendency to view areas of diversity as oppositional. For example, discourses around gender and health recognise that there are both health advantages and disadvantages to being male or female. A gender-inclusive approach takes gender from the margins of feminist activism to the mainstream of healthcare provision, while resisting binary categorisations (Annandale and Riska, 2009). Difference does not equate with conflict.

Despite methodological limitations, a similar pattern emerges from a study of diversity. Some groups in society are badly served by health services and similar findings emerge in areas other than pain. The most affected are those with multiple characteristics of disadvantage. These mirror disadvantage found in other areas of life – income inequality, poor education, etc. Many studies on diversity and pain have been conducted in emergency departments as it is here that poor pain relief is seen at its most stark. It is possible that in ward or community settings a more individual approach is taken, as patients and staff are able to enter into a longer and more personal relationship.

# CHAPTER SIX

# Pain as a Contested Experience

As we saw in Chapter 3, pain is experienced subjectively and yet attempts to quantify it by the use of pain scales are very common in healthcare settings. Using numerical or visual scales, patients are asked to communicate their pain to health professionals. However, such ways of viewing pain, while seeming to provide some sort of objective measure, merely serve to marginalise those whose pain does not fit into the biomedical or psychological models. This chapter will consider those whose pain is marginalised, and the way they describe their own experience and make sense of it in the context of their lives. Many people never discover a cause for their pain, which remains unexplained. Others may receive a diagnosis that is viewed with some degree of scepticism within both the medical profession and the lay population. The consequences of being diagnosed with a contested disease or labelled as suffering from 'unexplained pain' will be explored by way of qualitative studies. The ways that people respond to this, for example by striving to be viewed as credible patients, will also be considered.

## What do we mean by 'contested' and 'unexplained'?

In Chapter 2 we discussed Parsons' concept of 'the sick role', and in particular its implications for long-term illness and pain. The aspect of Parsons' theory that is crucial for understanding 'contested' and 'unexplained' illness is its identification of the power that the medical profession has over the legitimation of illness, and the influence this has over how the lay population perceives it.

An illness is contested when there is no general acceptance around what it is, what causes it, or even whether it exists at all. There may be a cultural element to this; for example, in Germany low blood pressure (hypotension) is considered a medical condition that needs treatment to bring it to within 'normal' limits, whereas in other countries it is considered a variation of normal. Some physicians now treat a condition known as 'pre-diabetes' (identified with marginally raised blood glucose levels) with medication in the hope of avoiding some of the complications of diabetes, but there is no evidence that this is preferable to dietary and lifestyle changes. Moreover, what was considered a risk factor is elevated to the status of 'pre-disease', thereby medicalising large numbers of healthy people. The debate over where the parameters of 'normal' lie is often at the heart of what makes something contested. Within biomedicine there are often norms derived from robust research that guide doctors into categorising a blood test result or a patient's weight, for example, as 'normal' or 'abnormal', but these are constructs, and not absolutes.

Very often a cluster of symptoms may occur in a number of people, but the cause of the symptoms remains elusive. The trajectory of the disease and the prognosis remain poorly understood. Measurable medical classification and patient experience are at odds. Yet identifiable causes of illness and their subsequent legitimation are what turn a contested illness into a socially acceptable one. The label of 'unexplained symptoms' or illness is usually applied when all relevant biomedical investigations have been conducted without a cause being found, and therefore no diagnostic label is given. In women who experience chronic pelvic pain (CPP), for example, some may be diagnosed with endometriosis (but as we will see later in this chapter and in Chapter 8, this diagnosis may also prove problematic) or with pelvic inflammatory disease, but for around 35 per cent their symptoms will remain unexplained

(McGowan et al., 2010). This may be relatively unproblematic in the case of a short-lived or self-limiting condition, but for those who live with long-term illness the lack of explanation, and their inability to make sense of what is happening to their body, can impact negatively on their lives, and the lives of those around them.

The contested or unexplained nature of illness stems from the inability of modern medicine to name and explain what is happening, when none of the usual diagnostic tools, such as blood tests or X-rays, can provide satisfactory answers. A name may be given to a collection of symptoms following the exclusion of other explanations, yet this is a negative rather than a positive categorisation, as is the label 'non-specific', which again signifies a lack of certainty. Yet as biomedicine has become hegemonic in matters of health and illness, so the expectation of what it can deliver has increased. Furthermore, as Western societies, and increasingly the rest of the world, have bestowed on the medical profession the power of legitimation of illness, there are serious economic and social consequences for people whose illness cannot be legitimised. Health professionals are considered to be impartial experts whose diagnosis 'labels, defines, and predicts and, in doing so, helps constitute and legitimate the reality that it discerns' (Rosenberg, 2002: 240). We can explore this more fully by considering some examples from research on the experience of contested or unexplained illness.

## Contested illness

In the mid-1980s reports began to emerge within medical practice of a collection of symptoms that usually included fatigue and exhaustion, muscle pain and a degree of memory disturbance. This set of symptoms became known at the time as chronic fatigue syndrome (CFS), but subsequently the nomenclature altered as theories about the aetiology emerged and then fell out of favour. The commonly used term at present is myalgic encephalopathy (ME). Reflecting the contested nature of the illness, national bodies responsible for naming and defining diseases have come to different conclusions about the classification of the symptoms (Walker, 2012). So, the Centre for Disease Control in the USA states that in order to be diagnosed with ME individuals need to experience significant fatigue lasting more than six months, accompanied by at least four of seven symptoms (concentration/memory impairment, sore throat, muscle/joint pain, swollen lymph nodes, headaches, unrefreshing sleep, post-exertional malaise). The stricter the defining factors of a disease, the more the definition conforms to a biomedical model, which may be useful for clinicians and researchers, but less so for patients who may fail to meet all of the conditions set and so be left without an explanation or legitimation of their symptoms (Walker, 2012). The problem for patients is compounded by the fact that everyone feels fatigue at times, and by media stories that dismiss the condition with the use of terms such as 'yuppie flu'. In his review into research on chronic illness, the sociologist Mike Bury notes that some conditions 'may produce symptoms, which because of their widespread occurrence in milder forms, among the normal [sic] population, make legitimation extremely difficult' (1991: 456). As will become apparent in later examples in this section, the existence of similar but milder symptoms within the wider population can be problematic for people experiencing contested illness, and may lead to accusations of malingering and to stigmatisation.

In a study from Sweden, Åsbring and Närvänen (2004) interviewed twenty-five women diagnosed with either CFS (the term used by the authors) or fibromyalgia, a condition characterised by widespread pain. Like CFS, fibromyalgia is a contested illness with symptoms that vary between people, and within the same person at different times. Furthermore, the trajectory and prognosis is not predictable. The study used an interactionist approach to explore the relative power relationships between the participants and their healthcare providers in terms of the strategies employed by the women to shift power and control in their favour. The women viewed the acquisition of knowledge through reading widely and consulting a range of sources on causes and treatments as an important method for gaining control. Their aim was to find an explanation for their symptoms, and to seek out a diagnosis and possible treatments to effect some improvement. They also became knowledgeable about the healthcare system, which they felt enabled them to exercise some control over their treatment by influencing healthcare providers. Some of the women used power strategies to try and influence the process, such as disengaging with their current care provider and changing doctor, or refusing to comply with the prescribed treatment and demanding alternative treatments. The women with CFS tended to use power strategies more than the women with fibromyalgia, and the authors suggest this may have been because they had a higher level of education which may have equipped them to resist social control by health professionals. Some women, however, reported that feeling so ill and/or in pain made them less able to assert themselves during medical encounters, and the diffuse nature of their symptoms gave health professionals the opportunity to invalidate their experiences. Interestingly (and unusually), Åsbring and Närvänen also interviewed the women's physicians in their study, and their perspectives on the patients will be discussed in Chapter 8.

Despite the fact that fibromyalgia is diagnosed by exclusion, and is contested by a sceptical medical profession, a drug treatment has been approved for use by the Federal Drug Administration (FDA) in the USA, and also adopted elsewhere. As Kristin Barker (2011) notes, the development and approval of a biomedical treatment presupposes the existence of the condition to be treated. So the prescription of the drug Pregabalin (Lyrica) not only represents a therapeutic hope, but is also a symbolic victory in validating those who have suffered in pain. Developments such as this have shifted the role of the

pharmaceutical industry from being solely a provider of treatments to becoming an engine of diagnosis, largely through
direct-to-consumer advertising (DTCA) of prescription medication. Although this is only currently allowed in the United
States and New Zealand, the internet provides a vehicle for
wider dissemination to patients in other countries. The pharmaceutical industry now has the cultural authority to define
disease, in a way only doctors had in the past. Examples of this
include the development of Prozac (a powerful antidepressant)
for anxiety or panic attacks, or Viagra for impotence which also
medicalises healthy men's sexual performance. This is in stark
contrast to the stance taken in the past by Parsons (see Chapter
3) and Friedson (Chapter 8), which positions the medical profession as being hegemonic in control over diagnosis.

The argument follows that if a medication helps a condition,
then that condition must be a medical disease. If the medication works on the central nervous system (CNS), then the
disease must be a disease of the CNS. As Barker states: 'DTCA
encourages the belief that there is "a pill for every ill" and,
increasingly, "an ill for every pill"' (2011: 835). Lyrica provides
a medical explanation for symptoms, and a corroboration of
fibromyalgia as a biomedical condition, as well as treatment.
However, this is a double-edged sword, as the DTCA for Lyrica
gives an unrealistic picture of living with fibromyalgia and of
the effectiveness of the drug. So now, while the general population can believe in the illness, which reduces stigmatisation
of the condition for the sufferer, it also expects sufferers to be
'cured' by Lyrica. This has the unwanted effect of discrediting the sufferer and therefore increasing stigmatisation when
the cure does not occur. So the pharmaceutical industry may
validate a condition while at the same time it discredits the
individual (Barker, 2011).

The formal criteria for diagnosis of fibromyalgia – three
months widespread pain, and tenderness in at least eleven of
eighteen locations on the body, the so-called 'tender points'
– do not correspond to any anatomical structure, nor does

tenderness in these locations correspond to any observable pathology (Barker, 2011). However, even where diagnostic criteria are fulfilled this does not necessarily mean that a disease is uncontested. Endometriosis is a disease of the female reproductive system in which tissue normally located in the uterus is found within the wider reproductive organs, the peritoneum, and even the rest of the abdominal cavity. It has even on rare occasions been located in the lungs or brain. These deposits respond to the hormonal cycle and bleed during menstruation in places from which the blood cannot escape, causing the typical symptom of chronic abdominal pain during menstruation. In qualitative research women give graphic descriptions of their pain as being 'like a knife', 'glass cutting through me', or 'nails clawing your stomach' (Denny, 2004a). Lesions may be seen on scans or MRI, and a cancer antigen (CA125) may be raised, although definitive diagnosis can only be made by visualising lesions at laparoscopy, and through histological assessment of biopsies (Denny, 2009a).

Following a diagnosis, endometriosis remains a contested disease, and although there are areas of similarity with CFS/ ME and fibromyalgia, it is problematic for different reasons. In a critical review of the literature on endometriosis, Culley et al. (2013b) found that women experienced a significant delay in receiving a diagnosis. Ballard et al. (2006) categorise this in terms of both patient delays and doctor delays. As the predominant symptom of endometriosis is abdominal pain during menstruation, many women feel that their experience is 'normal', or that they somehow cannot cope as other women do, and therefore they do not immediately seek medical help (Marcovic et al., 2008), or they struggle to distinguish 'normal' from 'pathological' (Toye et al., 2014). For those who do seek help, doctor delays occur when their symptoms are normalised, or dismissed as 'women's problems' and no further action is taken. They also find themselves misdiagnosed with irritable bowel disease (IBD) or pelvic inflammatory disease (PID), and referred for inappropriate secondary care (Jones et al., 2004).

This is compounded by the fact that the extent of endometriotic lesions does not necessarily correlate with the amount of pain experienced, so some women have extensive endometriosis which is only discovered coincidentally, whereas others experience severe pain from minimal disease. As one woman reported: 'He [the GP] obviously had no idea how this disease can affect you at all. He told me, "You've only got spots of [endometriosis], lots of women have that and they get on with their life"' (Denny, 2009a: 991). Endometriosis is also bound up with menstruation, which tends to be considered private and is not openly discussed in many societies, so women may actively conceal their problems, in particular from men (Seear, 2009). Endometriosis may impact on all aspects of a woman's life. Education and employment may be disrupted by constant sickness absence, social activities are often curtailed leading to the loss of friends, and a strain is put on relationships (Denny, 2004a; Huntington and Gilmour, 2005; Culley et al., 2013a).

As with many other contested conditions, there are treatments for endometriosis, which have varying degrees of success and may provide relief for a greater or lesser time. As Bury (1991) notes, a new crisis of credibility may occur, despite previous legitimation, if an individual continues to experience symptoms after their share of attention has been used up, for example following supposedly successful treatment. This may in turn close off support systems. As one participant put it: 'I think the doubting is the worst thing. Because it makes you feel like you're a liar or you are making more of it than perhaps you should' (Denny, 2004b: 42).

## What makes these illnesses contested?

Although the category of contested illness covers a range of symptoms and diagnoses, there are various themes that weave through many of the descriptions and individual stories. One of the most striking aspects of contested illness (and of unexplained illness, discussed in the next section) is gender, which was explored in Chapter 5. Here it is sufficient to reiterate that women report more painful conditions, more chronic symptoms and more loss of function than men. They also use more over-the-counter and prescription medication. Of course, some of the contested illnesses we considered above, such as endometriosis, are gendered, but even where this is not the case, women seem to be more prevalent in studies. This reason could be artefactual, as women may just be more likely to engage with research than men, but the epidemiological data are consistent with the assertion that women report more long-term pain than men (Nahin, 2015).

Also common to the descriptions is the discordance between biomedical evidence and patient experience. In Eccleston et al.'s (1997) comparative study of patients' and health professionals' accounts of pain the patients resisted the idea of non-physical causes of pain and deflected blame for not finding a cause onto the professionals. The professionals also deflected blame by viewing chronic pain as something learnt, and caused by poor pain management or bad advice in the past. An explanation of pain may be given via pharmaceutical efficacy – in other words, if pain is reduced by a treatment for a specific condition then it must be caused by that condition – but this does not diminish discordance or scepticism, as it is a negative rather than a positive deduction.

The final similarity is a well-documented delay in diagnosis. When symptoms can be caused by a range of diseases, or are quite common, it can be difficult to ascribe a definitive cause. Individuals delay seeking medical help as they may not think their symptoms serious, and doctors may refer inappropriately, or not take the symptoms seriously.

## Unexplained symptoms/illness

Whereas in contested illness a diagnosis is given, albeit with debate about whether what is diagnosed even constitutes a physical condition, for some people their pain remains unexplained despite many attempts to discover its cause. From our discussion in Chapter 3 on the sick role, it is evident that having their illness legitimised is important for people, and provides currency within healthcare and welfare systems. The proliferation of diagnostic procedures has increased the apparent certainty with which health professionals may match a patient's symptoms with a visible pathology within the body, or provide a quantitative measure that can be compared to an accepted norm (Denny, 2010). Rhodes et al. (2002) argue that two related assumptions inform both lay and professional understandings of the body under investigation. First, that what is happening within the body corresponds to the visual images of it, and this view of the body is objective and 'true'. Second, that measuring variations of the body against a norm can show what is typical and what is deviant. As we saw in Chapter 1, this way of viewing the body is a recent phenomenon, and one that leaves people whose symptoms remain unexplained after exhaustive medical testing feeling frustrated and let down.

The label of medically unexplained symptoms (MUS) is applied to 'those patients who have symptoms that have no identified organic basis' (Nettleton, 2006b: 1168). Nettleton further notes that this was initially a description rather than a label, and that there is now an attempt to differentiate between those people with MUS who have mental health problems, classified as 'somatisers', and those who do not. Despite this differentiation, Nettleton observes, there are many references to psychological factors in MUS discourse. Sharpe defines MUS as 'symptoms that are disproportionate to identifiable physical disease' (2001: 501). This definition implies that an objective judgement can be made about correct or appropriate levels of pain for specific diseases or levels of pathology. In reality such judgements are highly subjective (Denny, 2009a). Bendelow (2009a) observes that although symptoms that cannot be explained pathologically are low on the medical hierarchy, the MUS label is nevertheless less stigmatising than one of psychosomatic illness, so may be preferred by patients. In her study with patients with unexplained neurological symptoms, Nettleton (2006b) also found that they resisted psychological labels. Many patients, however, just want an explanation, an answer to the question 'how come I have this pain?' (Grace and MacBride-Stewart, 2007). When symptoms remain unexplained people are reluctant to disclose them to others in case they are viewed as hypochondriacs, whereas they are more likely to disclose a diagnosed illness (Charmaz, 2010). A Danish study on MUS patients reported that in the early stages what the author terms 'the symptomatic idiom' (the use of vocabulary that is common currency within a community) is dominant in consultations with GPs, but as time goes on this seems to lose significance and other explanations (social, moral and personal) take over, as people try to make sense of their symptoms in the context of their lives (Risør, 2009: 505).

One type of pain that is very common and for which a diagnosis is often not forthcoming is low back pain, despite the existence of many imaging techniques that can visualise the spinal column. Rhodes and colleagues (2002) explored chronic back pain sufferers' experience of pain, self-care and medical treatment in the USA. The patients' narratives of their experience almost always included diagnostic testing, both as something that was done to them by health professionals over which they had no control and as something which they actively sought. When visual imaging corresponded with the experience of pain the patients were satisfied. As one person commented: 'I felt relieved. I felt, like, here's proof. It's not just me going crazy or complaining. It's black and white and anybody can see it' (Rhodes et al., 2002: 38). This comment is typical of those who have spent many years searching for answers, often from a sceptical medical profession. Those patients who do not find a cause for their pain continue to put their faith in medical knowledge to legitimise it, viewing failure as the fault of individual doctors, rather than the biomedical system itself. However, as we saw in Chapter 4, some people will eventually disengage from formal services.

A common thread running through all of these studies is that of gaining legitimation and being accepted as genuine. A Norwegian study continues this theme by arguing that people with chronic back pain strive to achieve the sick role in order to have their pain accepted as real, and not be accused of malingering, hypochondria or mental illness; as one participant put it: 'Because then you've got a piece of paper saying "you are sick"' (Glenton, 2003: 2243). However, access to the sick role is not necessarily sufficient to convince friends and family that one's illness is genuine, and even health professionals may have only partially legitimated the pain in the absence of tangible 'proof', so participants may still feel stigmatised. Glenton (2003) argues that the expectations of the sick role are unrealistic for people living with low back pain, but rather than challenge them her participants attempted to live up to these expectations in order to reap the benefits of gaining access.

A good deal of ambivalence emerges from the narratives of people with MUS (Nettleton, 2006b). Patients did not want to have a 'disease', yet they wanted to be cured. They wanted diagnostic tests to reveal something that could be cured, but dreaded finding out that they have something incurable or life-threatening. Nettleton describes these patients as 'medical orphans' as they feel marginalised by the medical profession and 'all at sea' as a result of being passed from one specialist to another (2006c: 208). Interestingly, Nettleton also suggests that people with MUS may be less well served today than when medicine was less developed, as 'doctors may be less skilled in providing support and ongoing care against a background of diagnostic uncertainty' (2006c: 209).

## Uncertainty

'To have pain is to have *certainty*; to hear about pain is to have *doubt*' (Scarry, 1985: 13). Contested illness and unexplained symptoms are frequently accompanied by uncertainty on a number of levels. Indeed, a recurring theme throughout this book is the idea that any pain experienced over a long period may be associated with a greater or lesser degree of uncertainty. Uncertainty in long-term illness may be categorised in terms of diagnostic uncertainty, symptomatic uncertainty and trajectory uncertainty (Williams, 2000: 44). This can be evidenced by Denny's (2009a) research, which, as highlighted above, demonstrated how the experience of endometriosis is bound up with uncertainty throughout the whole of the illness trajectory. To recap, women with this disease typically experience a delay of many years in receiving a diagnosis, either because they perceive their symptoms as normal or as something to be endured, and therefore do not seek medical help, or because health professionals do not take them seriously. They report being 'fobbed off' by doctors, and frequently describe their efforts to be taken seriously as a battle or struggle (Denny and Mann, 2008). Symptomatic uncertainty is exacerbated by the fact that many women experience symptoms similar to those of endometriosis and yet do not have the disease. Conversely some women with severe disease experience no symptoms and are only diagnosed opportunistically. Trajectory uncertainty occurs as there is no known cure for endometriosis, and even following seemingly successful treatment the course of the disease is unpredictable and it frequently reoccurs. Although endometriosis can be debilitating, and impact on every aspect of a woman's life, it is of little interest to the medical profession or to the wider public, and so receives scant attention. As one woman in Denny's study commented: 'It's not a sexy disease. It's not life-threatening so there is very little interest' (Denny, 2009a: 989–90).

Compounding the uncertainty may be the addition of 'non-specific' to the disease label, which can make it difficult for the sufferer to accept the pain and to redefine 'self' and 'biography'. A study with people with low back pain showed that use of the labels 'non-specific' or 'pain of unknown origin' meant that participants did not know the nature of their pain, which they considered to be a necessary condition to accepting it as chronic, and for making adaptions to their lives (Corbett et al., 2007). The uncertainty left people fluctuating between hope and despair. Hope is signified in the expectation of diagnosis, treatment and resolution occurring as a linear process, but also in the adjustment of priorities. Despair results from persistent pain leading to feelings of hopelessness and the envisaging of an inevitable increase in levels of pain. Sufferers fluctuated between these two states. They could not construct a frame of reference for the nature and course of their condition against which to plot their own trajectory in order to achieve a semblance of certainty. The unknown cause and uncertain nature of their pain resulted in participants fearing for the future, making planning for daily life and future employment difficult. However, turning points from hope to despair and vice versa not only revolved around levels of pain but were also bound up with perceptions of control and identity, which in turn were associated with social context (Corbett et al., 2007).

Christopher Adamson (1997) drew on his experience of inflammatory bowel disease (IBD) and avascular necrosis (AVN) to identify two forms of uncertainty – existential (a key aspect of the illness experience) and clinical (referring to diagnosis and treatment) – and how these mutually affected each other. Keeping a diary of his illness journey, he only later became aware that existential and clinical uncertainty were the main themes of the entries. IBD is a collective diagnosis for a range of bowel conditions characterised by bloody diarrhoea and abdominal cramp. One point of clinical uncertainty concerns which of these conditions is causing the patient's symptoms, which is important as treatment will be different in each case. Following both drug treatment, which did not improve the symptoms, and surgery, a definitive diagnosis still could not be given, but Adamson was told it was 'probably Crohn's disease'. Following this, AVN was misdiagnosed on several occasions as an arthritic condition, leaving Adamson in severe pain. Here the clinical uncertainty intensified the existential uncertainty, but this was reversed when a diagnosis of AVN was reached and experimental and uncertain surgery was recommended. By this stage, having achieved a degree of existential certainty following pain relief obtained by using crutches, Adamson now felt confident in questioning the advisability of the proposed treatment and seeking another opinion. He concludes that there is a philosophical gulf between the existential voice of the patient and the clinical voice of the clinician, and that neither voice can fully control the encounter, each being limited by the condition of 'pervasive uncertainty' (Adamson, 1997: 153).

## Being believed

As noted in the discussions above, people want to have their pain believed and to be taken seriously by clinicians. Reviews of the relevant literature suggest that being believed is a vital component of the pain assessment process, and of the relationship between health professionals and patients (Clarke and Iphofen, 2005), and that being disbelieved leads to stigma, isolation and emotional distress (Newton et al., 2013). For Glenton's (2003) participants their rationale for accessing the sick role was to have their pain believed, and many expressed the fear that those around them questioned the reality of their low back pain. As mentioned earlier in the discussion of Bury (1991), one of the difficulties in being believed is the widespread occurrence of many symptoms in milder forms among the general population. For example, most women will at some time experience menstrual pain, and low back pain is a common occurrence. For most people these conditions are short-lived and self-limiting. Knowing when and how the commonplace and the normal tips over into the abnormal and pathological is difficult, and appearing to 'get it wrong' can attract the stigmatising labels of malingering or hypochondria. Individuals may feel dismissed by care providers, and report frustration in their partners at their ongoing illness. One woman eventually diagnosed with an abdominal virus said of her husband: '[he] was getting frustrated with me. He couldn't believe that I felt sick all the time, and said it was all in my head' (Johnson and Johnson, 2006: 164). For someone living with pain, not being believed can lead to isolation as others distance themselves and delegitimise the pain. Sufferers may also isolate themselves and withdraw from social life to avoid stigmatisation (Richardson, 2005). Werner and Malterud (2003) found that women with unexplained pain experienced negative encounters with doctors and had to work at being taken seriously, using strategies such as preparing for the consultation, dressing in what they considered an appropriate manner, and trying to appear credible.

## Summary

Narrative research demonstrates the frustration felt by people who experience contested illness or MUS. Although this body of research is not generalisable, it is internally consistent, and provides insights into the lives of people who live with these conditions. Most of the conditions that come under the label of unexplained or contested are not life-threatening, and do not attract the interest of the medical profession in the same way as, say, cancer or coronary heart disease. The status of back pain, pelvic pain or rheumatic pain is low in the medical hierarchy, and often trivialised (Denny, 2009a). This is highlighted by the comment above that endometriosis is not a sexy disease. Living with pain or other disabling symptoms does, however, impact considerably on quality of life and can negatively affect education and work prospects, relationships and social life. Some conditions such as low back pain or endometriosis fluctuate in severity, making legitimation more difficult, and symptoms may be trivialised or psychologised by health professionals, friends and family, and even the sufferers themselves.

People may progress through a series of 'treatment rituals' which can often start with simple analgesia, proceed through more targeted drug treatments, and may end with surgery. As one treatment proves ineffective, so some hope is raised that the next may be successful. The lack of effective treatments often leads people onto the 'medical merry-go-round' (Robinson, 1988; Cox et al., 2003; Nettleton, 2006c), as they try to seek answers and practical and psychosocial support, although this term has been said to trivialise the very real suffering of individuals (Denny, 2009a). For many people an explanation is as important as a diagnosis.

MUS and contested illness is riddled with uncertainty, as most of these conditions do not have a clear trajectory (Corbett et al., 2007; Denny, 2009a). Uncertainty is usually experienced negatively in terms of living and working day to day, and in planning for the future, but for some of Corbett's participants it left open the possibility of a future cure. Uncertainty, even when coupled with some degree of hope, makes it difficult to construct a 'frame of reference' (Corbett et al., 2007: 1592) for the nature and course of an individual's condition. The experience of MUS and contested illness is illustrative of Frank's concept of the chaos narrative (see Chapter 3). Here there is no restitution. Events happen without any purpose or order; as the name implies, the plot is chaotic, unpredictable and random (Frank, 1995).

It should be noted here that the behaviours and actions attributed to clinicians in this chapter have been interpreted by patients taking part in research. Chapter 8 will look again at the issue of contested illness and unexplained conditions utilising research that focuses on the perspective of health professionals. Before doing so, however, we will turn to the issue of emotional pain.

# CHAPTER SEVEN

# Emotional Pain and Suffering

This chapter moves away from the focus on acute and long-term physical pain in order to consider emotional pain and suffering. My intention is not to imply a division between physical and emotional pain. As we have seen in previous chapters, in telling their stories people often fuse the two, and do not overtly think about compartmentalising their experience. As was discussed in Chapter 4, Cicely Saunders incorporated emotional pain and suffering into her concept of 'total pain', and viewed its relief as part of the work of the hospice movement. The emotional pain and suffering of individuals has also been apparent in many of the stories that have been cited throughout the book.

Here I want to highlight some of the recent sociological work that has sought to counteract the omission of non-medical perspectives from clinical research and practice and provide an insight into the world of those who suffer, in particular, from emotional pain. I will also expand on a theme that has been raised in previous chapters, but which has largely been treated unproblematically: the issue of the psychologising of pain. The chapter concludes with a description and critique of the biopsychosocial model that was developed in order to incorporate the non-medical aspects of pain in an integrated whole, and to move beyond the mind/body dualism.

## Emotions

Emotions have often been underplayed and undervalued in research, with efforts made to control for them, rather than conceptualising their components (Bendelow, 2000). Yet they are 'integral to our being. They can move us, subdue us, be a source of pain and pleasure and of information about the situations and relationships in which we find ourselves' (Freund, 1990: 453). Freund goes on to suggest that a holistic view of the body requires it to be studied as a living, acting entity.

Williams and Bendelow (1998) note that some postmodernist scholars have attempted to deconstruct essentialism, the mind/body dualism, and interior/exterior ideas of the self – in short, the binary divisions underpinning some sociological thinking. While this work is important, it has also served to dematerialise the body, and to prioritise the 'social'. An anti-dualist approach through embodiment (see Chapter 2), Williams and Bendelow inform us, can move the debate forward by interfusing mind and body, reason and emotion, and pleasure and pain. This is captured by the idea of 'the lived body' (Vrancken, 1989: 441), in which the exterior, objective body is not treated as different from the inner sensations of the subjective body, providing a focus for the sociology of pain as 'an "embodied" emotional and affective experience' (Williams and Bendelow, 1998: 135). In day-to-day life the relationship we have with our body is 'taken for granted' and barely thought about; we vacillate between being and having a body. For the person in pain, 'I' and 'my body' become two separate things; the pain makes us believe we can cut ourselves off from our bodies (Vrancken, 1989: 442). So we cannot dispose of dualisms altogether, and at an experiential level the person in pain will objectify their body. Emotion may provide a 'missing link' that has the potential to bridge mind and body, individual and society (Williams and Bendelow, 1998: 137). As we have discussed earlier in this book, fear, anger, despair and other emotions all contribute to the experience of physical pain. Dunham et al. (2013), for example, have noted the complex relationship between emotions and the pain of cancer, bound up with feelings of helplessness and vulnerability.

Kleinman and Seeman report the response of a mother

who had been asked to complete a questionnaire concerning the effect of her son's muscular dystrophy on the family. She responded: 'I sometimes think we are all dying, not just Andy [her son]. Even my parents and brothers and sisters have been more than "affected"' (2000: 231). She goes on to tell of her family: a husband who resorted to drink and then disappeared, and her two other children who experienced guilt (because they were 'normal') and intense anger at their mother that they could not express, as she had been absorbed in Andrew's care. This vignette demonstrates the destructive ripple effect of a life-threatening illness on the lifeworld of the family and 'on the bodily and emotional health of its members' (Kleinman and Seeman, 2000: 231).

Implicit in this story is the emotion work carried out by the mother in managing the needs of the family and keeping it together. Exley and Letherby (2001) found that people with infertility/involuntary childlessness or terminal illness engaged in a lot of emotion work in order to maintain relationships. This was true of close relationships, but also involved more casual relationships, such as those with work colleagues, as well. It could be carried out on and for the self, such as avoiding friends with new babies, or on and for others. For example, one woman who was terminally ill spoke of sorting things out for the family, and preparing them for her death. Emotion work was a way of reaffirming the identities of participants as still part of the mainstream and not just the 'infertile' or 'terminally ill' person.

## Suffering

We tend to use words like 'pain' and 'suffering' quite loosely in general speech, as if we have a shared meaning. Yet, as Wilkinson informs us, although we can recognise and respond to the outward signs of distress in others, we can never 'enter into the realms of their personal experience of suffering' (2005: 16). Suffering is uniquely our own, which makes it hard to agree on a definition. Lasch (2005) points out that in talking of suffering we use a verb, 'to suffer', which implies agency, but in talking of pain we use a noun preceded by a preposition, 'in pain', with connotations of causality – 'something caused my pain'. The distinction between pain and suffering is often taken to differentiate the physiological sensation of pain from the psychological response to it, reflecting the mind/body dualism, and locating pain within the realms of biomedicine. However, Wilkinson points to the extent to which pain, particularly chronic pain, also reflects the personal distress arising from the social frustrations and personal contradictions with which people are obliged to live, rather than pathology or injury. The pain of suffering can take many forms; for example, participants in one study spoke of aching loneliness, and the pain of not mattering any longer in their old age (van Wijngaarden et al., 2015).

Hydén, whose typology of narrative was explored in Chapter 4, states that 'one of our most powerful forms for expressing suffering and experiences related to suffering is the narrative. Patients' narratives give voice to suffering in a way that lies outside the domain of the biomedical voice' (1997: 49). In telling stories about their illness, people are also showing what it is like to suffer, and those who witness that suffering, such as family and health professionals, also produce narratives (Radley, 2005). Bearing witness to the suffering of someone else involves more than just reporting on it; it is also the storyteller's account of their reaction to hearing about the suffering.

Rather than try to define or conceptualise suffering, some commentators have focused on the circumstances under which it takes place, such as following a loss or bereavement, or an experience of social isolation or injustice, and how it is manifested, for example in depression, anxiety or humiliation. Studies of patients with cancer suggest that suffering is the interplay between the physical symptoms like pain or fatigue, depression, and the ensuing withdrawal and social isolation (Ellis et al., 2015).

On the other hand, Arthur Frank argues that suffering is indefinable because it is the reality of what is not. He continues: 'Suffering is the unspeakable, as opposed to what can be spoken; it is what remains concealed, impossible to reveal; it remains in darkness, eluding illumination; and it is dread, beyond what is tangible even if hurtful' (2001: 355). One response to the difficulty in articulating suffering is to remain silent, and an area where silence has traditionally been the norm is that of intimate partner violence (IPV). Here we can recognise the salience of Frank's words, as women and men struggle to maintain an outward normality. A study of West African women in heterosexual relationships in Australia described how women would laugh and keep up the pretence of a happy relationship to the outside world while experiencing physical violence and suffering in silence (Ogunsiji et al., 2012). Although violence against women by men is considered a serious public health problem, violence within same-sex relationships and violence at older ages receive less attention and are often thought not to constitute a major problem. In these cases the violence may be more likely to remain hidden due to the abused partner's perceived shame and stigma and a feeling that they will not be believed, or because of a dependence on the perpetrator (McKenry et al., 2006; McGarry et al., 2010).

A British study of forty-nine people with cancer attending palliative care services found that, although they were near the end of life, not all participants felt themselves to be suffering. For those who did, there was a range of ideas as to what this meant, and how it affected them. Some patients perceived suffering as a normal part of life, and inevitable during terminal illness. Others viewed it as either avoidable or unavoidable, physical or emotional, or bound up with loss. Some patients experienced a transformation through suffering, gaining a new understanding of themselves (Ellis et al., 2015). As this study was carried out at a hospice day centre, the patients' views may have been influenced by the attention to end-of-life issues given by the centre, but the findings are consistent with

Wilkinson's in that the suffering experienced was unique to each person.

A different approach to suffering among people with cancer was found by Saarnio et al. (2012). In this study, the experience of suffering influenced power relations within an individual's social context and vice versa. People in a vulnerable social group experienced increased suffering in addition to living with cancer. Multiple power relations and feelings based on gender, age, ethnicity and educational level were found to influence the experience of suffering for this group. This was manifest in frustration, a subordinated social position, and feelings of guilt, among other things. Conversely, middle-aged men with high educational levels were not seen to have unique patterns of suffering or to adopt a suffering identity, but rather experienced feelings of control and expressed satisfaction with health services (Saarnio et al., 2012).

In developing the debate around a sociology of suffering, Wilkinson argues that we need to give more attention to the ways in which people encounter and give voice to suffering. Further, since societies are failing to acknowledge how suffering affects people, there is a need to reflect upon the cultural discourse used to communicate the social meanings of personal affliction, 'so as to take note of the ways in which these may be designed (sometimes quite deliberately) to "silence" the voices of people in extremes of hardship and pain' (Wilkinson, 2005: 167).

## Mental health

A number of issues we have looked at around gender disadvantage and health have focused on the experience of women and pain. Women receive a mental (ill-)health diagnosis more often than men for conditions such as depression, anxiety and eating disorders, and attend out-patient mental health services more often than men (Rogers and Pilgrim, 2010). In a classic study, Brown and Harris (1978) identified factors that for the first time pointed to depression having social origins. Loss of mother before the age of eleven years, lack of a confidante, and three or more children at home were all said to be linked with a depressive illness in women. These authors accepted formal psychiatric definitions in their study, and the factors identified were associations, which could not point to a causative mechanism. Despite these limitations, more recent work by Brown and Harris and others has also made similar links between social factors and depression in women (see, for example, Kessler and Bromet, 2013).

Being male also has consequences for how emotions are dealt with and is a factor in suicide rates, which are higher among men. The highest suicide rate in the UK is for men aged forty-five to forty-nine, at 26.5 per 100,000, followed by men aged thirty to forty (Samaritans, 2016). Although younger men have lower rates of suicide, as death is uncommon in the young in industrialised nations, it is the leading cause of death among twenty- to thirty-four-year-olds, representing 24 per cent of all deaths in this age group. Chapter 5 highlighted how masculinity influenced men's views on illness and their subsequent behaviour, and this is among the factors of importance in mental health and suicide.

A report commissioned by the Samaritans describes suicide as an individual act that takes place within a specific social, economic and cultural context. Although the social context has changed since Durkheim's study of suicide in 1897 (see Chapter 1), the concept of both internal and external factors playing a part has endured. Wylie et al. (2012) attempted to explain why middle-aged men of lower socio-economic status are so vulnerable to death by suicide. Although there are many psychological and personality factors involved, socio-economic factors around masculine roles and scripts are also implicated. Low socio-economic status makes it harder for men to fulfil the hegemonic masculine role of the breadwinner, and to adapt to new forms of work not based on manual labour. Men who judge themselves against a masculine 'gold standard' that

values power, control and invincibility may well fall short, leading to feelings of shame and worthlessness (Wylie et al., 2012:
1). A literature review on men and mental health found similar
factors at work, but also commented on the lack of good-quality
supporting evidence (Robertson et al., 2015). However, it did
report a relationship between adherence to traditional forms
of masculinity and poorer mental health help-seeking, higher
levels of mental health stigma, and suicide attempts.

## Psychologising pain

In the absence of a diagnosis Grace notes that, 'When "nothing
is found", no real basis for the pain can be identified, the spec-
tre of psychological causation takes on a shadowy prospect'
(2003: 42), although none of the participants in her research
with women experiencing chronic pelvic pain knew what
this meant beyond the assumption that they were neurotic.
Similarly, women with endometriosis resist psychological
labels, wanting their symptoms to attract a biomedical diagnosis, to be followed by medical or surgical treatment (Denny,
2009a).

Psychologising illness or symptoms is the practice of
attributing them to psychological factors in the absence of supporting evidence. In the clinical setting this may be because
an organic basis cannot be found using existing diagnostic
methods, but it may also occur before any investigation takes
place. Although men are not immune, the majority of cases
of psychologisation in the literature have to do with women
(Goudsmit, 1994). The question here is why it is that people
view labels inferring a psychological basis for pain so negatively, and as not real. A clue can be found in another study
with women with endometriosis, one of whom commented:
'I was actually convinced by a doctor that I was psychosomatic
and a bit of a hypochondriac' (Denny, 2004b: 41). Similarly,
a woman in the 'resignation group' in Bendelow's study
of pain clinics (see Chapter 4) reported: 'My GP told me I

was imagining it, that I was being neurotic because the kids had left home' (1996: 178). The proliferation of laboratory tests and investigations may lead some health professionals to interpret a lack of clinical evidence for a patient's symptoms as evidence of the existence of a psychological cause. The hegemony of the biomedical model renders other explanations somehow inferior, and the term 'psychosomatic' is often linked in the minds of most clinicians and lay people with hypochondria. As a result, people seeking reassurance that their pain is real are having it questioned and can end up being viewed as either exaggerating or inventing the pain. This thinking only reinforces the mind/body dualism: if pain does not have a biological basis that can be identified, then it must be psychosomatic, a label that makes women more determined to find a respectable medical categorisation (Grace, 2003). A more straightforward reason for not wanting a psychological label is that finding a somatic reason for pain could result in treatment and prevent further suffering (Bendelow and Williams, 1996).

The nineteenth-century notion of the 'hysterical woman' was highlighted in Chapter 1, and similar stereotypes continue to operate today, with ambiguous chronic illnesses that are difficult to diagnose being 'feminized, trivialized, and dismissed by healthcare providers as psychological in origin' (Johnson and Johnson, 2006: 161). It is no accident that the examples above all involve women, as it is they who most frequently find themselves the subjects of psychologising. As noted in Chapter 4, the staff in the pain clinic described by Bendelow were reported as feeling that women were more likely to report pain and let it dominate their lives, although this was not borne out by the data (Bendelow and Williams, 1996). Other research has reported that middle-aged female patients are more likely than men to be construed as overly neurotic and requiring mild tranquillisers, and that distressed women (but not men) who were in work were advised to resign from their jobs (Rogers and Pilgrim, 2010).

## Infertility

In Chapter 5 it was noted that for some women with endometriosis the major issue is not the experience of pain but the possibility or reality of infertility. For many years the inability of a couple to reproduce was laid at the door of the female partner, and seen as a private trouble and a cause for pity. Technological changes from the 1960s onwards had the effect of bringing the issue into sharp focus, and giving the impression that fertility is totally under personal control. First, the development of the oral contraceptive gave women more control over fertility, and led to reproduction being seen as a choice rather than an inevitability. Second, assisted reproductive technologies, beginning with in vitro fertilisation (IVF) in 1978, meant that more help was available for infertile couples, and once a technology becomes available there follows an imperative to use it. The failure to reproduce thus became reconceptualised as a medical issue, and as a problem to be fixed by technology (this idea of infertility as a medical problem, for which reproductive technologies are the 'fix', has been comprehensively analysed and challenged – but that debate is beyond the scope of this volume). In order to understand the pain of infertility it is useful to consider the meaning of reproduction within society. Most societies are pro-natalist, that is, women (and to a lesser extent men) gain status through their ability to reproduce, and there is an expectation that adults will marry and will have children. When this life trajectory is not followed it results in the biographical disruption of an expected future, often leading to feelings of loss and despair. So infertility can be seen to be socially constructed, as it is shaped not merely by the absence of a pregnancy but also by societal expectations of marriage, childbearing, relatedness and family, as well as the availability of medical procedures to alleviate childlessness (Hudson and Culley, 2015). Whiteford and Gonzalez (1995: 28) call infertility 'a secret stigma', as it is invisible yet strongly felt by the woman or couple affected.

They contrast the medicalised infertility story of future interventions and new procedures with women's narratives of failure, stigma and spoiled identity.

The success rate for IVF has remained at around 30 per cent for some years, which means that for most couples attempting it a pregnancy and a baby will not be the outcome. Although other treatments may achieve more success, the expectations surrounding IVF and more recent reproductive technologies may still be unrealistically high. The emotional pain of infertility is compounded by the loss of an anticipated pregnancy through the procedure. As one woman stated: 'When I had a negative [pregnancy] test no one could have prepared me for how devastated I was going to feel. I just screamed and cried and was desperately upset' (Denny, 1993: 515). This research also reported feelings of guilt among women when embryos produced using IVF techniques failed to implant in their uterus, and they questioned whether they were responsible, or had subconsciously rejected them.

Most research on infertility has focused on women's experiences and emotions, to the exclusion of those of men. Indeed, Culley et al. have called men 'the "second sex" in reproduction research' (2013: 226). Men have described feeling marginalised and treated as onlookers during infertility investigations and treatments (Hinton and Miller, 2013). Not only has little attention been paid to men's reproductive experiences, little is also known about how male partners contribute to women's reproductive decision making. Where men have been studied it has been reported that they do not perceive infertility as negatively as women. However, this may reflect the way in which men and women are socialised to cope with negative experiences (Wischmann and Thorn, 2013), and other studies have found that infertility can be a major life crisis for men, associated with anxiety and distress (Culley et al., 2013). Male infertility also suffers from a fertility/virility link, whereby infertility is conflated with impotence in a way that female infertility is not (Hinton and Miller, 2013). Recently more attention has been paid to this, however, and a review of the literature found that men in less pro-natalist cultures, such as Denmark, suffered less psychological distress and were more open about their infertility than men living in countries where pro-natalist ideology was more pronounced (Wischmann and Thorn, 2013). These authors report that in other studies male factor infertility was associated with disbelief and denial, and a feeling of powerlessness that impacted on self-esteem and identity. Social expectations of masculinity are high, and as one respondent commented, 'There are male ideals which are propagated again and again, there is this template of the perfect male – and now I don't fit into this template anymore' (Wischmann and Thorn, 2013: 239). So a culture of pro-natalism may impact on men as well as women. The perception of men not conforming to societal norms of masculinity was also felt by their female partners, although the women's response to it tended to be different, expressing a need to share their emotions, whereas the men were focused on finding a way forward. This resonates with the different gender responses to living with endometriosis discussed in Chapter 5.

Primary research has mainly considered the expectations and experiences of women who have placed their infertility in the public domain by seeking medical solutions. There are, however, alternative perceptions of fertility and attitudes to motherhood that provide a lens through which to capture a broader picture. Letherby (1999) argues that once a woman has been defined as infertile, she is perceived as 'other', and will still fail to meet the 'ideal' of mother even if she subsequently bears children – whether as a result of technological intervention, or socially through adoption or fostering. In other words, women who have children by non-conventional means are seen as different from other mothers, in the same way as those who remain childless.

## The biopsychosocial model of pain

The biopsychosocial model began life as a response to the crisis of identity that taxed psychiatry during the 1970s. Was it analogous to medicine, and so needed to use the same language and values in order to diagnose and treat diseases of the brain, or was it a completely different discipline dealing with disorders of the mind, and having more in common with the behavioural sciences? George Engel, a professor of psychiatry and medicine, argued that a new model was required to unite both these opinions, but without 'sacrificing the enormous advantages of the medical model' (1977: 131). It would need to encompass a range of very different conditions, such as diabetes and schizophrenia, both as human experiences and as diseases. For while a chemical imbalance may indicate the presence of either of these conditions, it is not sufficient to explain the disease in individual patients. For that, as we have seen throughout this volume, it is crucial to take into account the individual's context and situation. Engel thus proposed the biopsychosocial (BPS) model, incorporating the cultural, social and psychological aspects of health and illness as well as the biological factors, where part of the doctor's task is to weigh up the relative contributions of each in a given situation.

> By evaluating all the factors contributing to both illness and patienthood, rather than giving primacy to biological factors alone, a biopsychosocial model would make it possible to explain why some individuals experience as 'illness' conditions which others regard merely as 'problems of living,' be they emotional reactions to life circumstances or somatic symptoms. (1977: 133)

Grace (2003) argues that the BPS model soon filled the vacuum created by concerns about explaining pain in terms of the mind/body dualism. Its proponents claim that it is the most heuristic (i.e., involving the use of experience to solve a problem, or what could be called a 'rule of thumb') model for evaluating and treating chronic pain currently available

(Gatchel, 2013). It is important to note that the BPS model involves more than just a mix of the individual elements; rather, it proposes a dynamic interaction between them, and cannot be broken down into its individual biological, psychological and social parts (Gatchel, 2013). Indeed, Grace and Zondervan (2006) further argue that within the model the biological and the psychosocial do not merely interact but co-produce pain.

For people with head and neck cancer (HNC), pain is a common occurrence, and the majority of patients experience it during radiotherapy treatment. Using a BPS model in order to understand the pain of HNC patients, Schaller et al. found that the interaction between the physical, psychological and social aspects of pain was not expressed by participants, who were all focused on the physical aspects of pain caused by the treatment, such as blisters: 'It burns on the tongue and it stings in the throat . . . It's like a sea of fire in the mouth' (2015: 339). While they did describe different aspects of pain – physical, psychological and social – they did not articulate a clear relationship between them. They were preoccupied with having a diagnosis of cancer, and being in pain. The authors conclude that the complexity of the BPS model, together with the dominance of the biomedical model, may prevent people from fully embracing it. This may be because, as Ghaemi (2011) has argued, the BPS model is too eclectic. He points to further limitations in terms of its lack of conceptualisation of a coherent relationship between mind and body, and its positivist characterisation of biology. On the other hand it has provided an important template for developing holistic and integrated models of healthcare which avoid outmoded mental/physical labels (Bendelow, 2009).

## Summary

Emotional pain and suffering are frequently left unexpressed or subsumed within physical pain. The voices of those experiencing such pain may remain unheard, and in particular the pain of those men who conform to traditional masculine scripts of being in control and remaining stoical may not be articulated. The responsibility for emotion work tends to be placed on the female in the family unit, usually the wife and mother, whose own emotional needs as carers are often left unmet. The biopsychosocial model of care attempts to overcome the binary of mind and body by incorporating the psychological and cultural with the biological, and although this has not been adopted uncritically, it does provide a template for the development of more holistic models of care. Despite more attention being paid to emotional pain and suffering in recent years, some people may continue to remain silent simply because they view such problems as part of life, or something to be endured, particularly as they get older. As in other chapters in this book, the concept of embodiment is important in exploring emotional pain and its accompanying suffering. The idea of the body as something an individual *is*, as well as something they *have*, provides a useful way of viewing the intersection of pain, suffering and emotion.

CHAPTER EIGHT

# Health Professionals' Perspectives on Pain

When people are in pain they may in the first instance try to manage it themselves with over-the-counter medication or devices such as TENS. They might set a time limit on how long they will endure the pain, or decide on the conditions under which they will seek medical help, for example if the pain becomes worse or starts to interfere with their ability to function. Eventually, if the pain is not self-limiting or relieved by easily accessible remedies, most people will seek medical help, and rely on the knowledge and experience of the clinician to provide a remedy. So clinicians are crucial in the way in which pain is defined and managed, and they also act as gatekeepers to other practitioners and health services that may relieve pain. Much research on pain, particularly chronic pain, is undertaken with the people who experience it, and it is their perspectives that are captured, including their views on how clinicians perceive them and their pain. Less sociological work has been conducted on the perspectives of health professionals themselves, and the way in which these may influence their management of patients, or the tensions that may be caused by differences between lay and professional interpretations of pain. It must be noted that the words 'doctor', 'health professional' or 'clinician' are being used here to refer to a social group, and individuals within that group will conform to or reject its norms and values to a greater or lesser extent. This distinction is important because there is not necessarily a correlation between the behaviour of practitioners and the institutional characteristics of the professional group to which they belong (Saks, 1995).

In Chapter 4 we looked at how health professionals behaved as practitioners; here we will think about them as a social group. This chapter will consider ways in which health professionals account for and interpret pain, the way their power is maintained and exerted, and how there may be a degree of dissonance between the meaning pain has for them and the meaning it has for their patients.

## Doctors as the legitimate experts in health and healing

In Chapters 3 and 4 the power of the medical profession to legitimate people's pain and to act as a gatekeeper to services and the sick role was discussed. This begs the question of how and why the medical profession and the biomedical model came to dominate the domain of pain. This may appear self-evident, but, as stated in Chapter 1, historically there were many forms of healers and the medical profession became pre-eminent because it was successful in gaining jurisdiction over the field of work that we now call healthcare. As Freidson reminds us, 'all healers are not called doctors or physicians, nor are they usually considered professionals in any other sense than that of making a living from their work (the opposite of amateurs)' (1970: 3). The 'medical gaze' (Foucault, 1973) was not the gaze of any healer, but the sanctioned gaze of the medical practitioner, who became hegemonic in the diagnosis and treatment of disease using the increasingly reductionist methods of clinical anatomy, and latterly biomedical sciences.

As we saw in Chapter 3, the concept of the sick role formed part of Talcott Parsons' systematic analysis of the medical profession. Within Parsons' functionalist approach the privileged position of medicine is a consequence of its functional significance for wider society in minimising sickness and hence the disruption it causes to society. This theoretical position emphasises the altruistic nature of medicine, viewing it as a profession with a strong collective ethic, working for the good of society rather than for personal gain. This approach has been accused of accepting uncritically the ideology professed by the profession itself, and others have argued that such privileged occupational groups do not subordinate their interests to those of wider society (Saks, 1995).

Taking a more critical approach, Freidson (1970) defines a profession as an occupation that has been successful in controlling its work, and which is sanctioned by the state through its legitimation of the profession's monopoly over certain tasks, including control over the requirements for entry into the profession itself. For Freidson, medicine constitutes the archetypal profession: it possesses great autonomy over its work and controls the work of other health occupations to a greater or lesser degree. Similarly, Parkin defines professionalism as a strategy of occupational closure, which limits and controls entrance to the occupation (what he terms social closure) in that professions exclude certain individuals or groups (such as women) from membership and from carrying out tasks over which it claims a monopoly (Parkin, 1974).

In industrialised Western societies the medical profession has become the acknowledged expert body in relation to health and disease, and has over time expanded its jurisdiction to cover many aspects of life that were once outside its scope. Some of these were considered in Chapter 4, but others come under the heading of the 'medicalisation of life' in that they are experiences that many people face at one time or another, such as childbirth, traumatic stress, the menopause or eating disorders. As well as recognition by the state, professionals also need a general recognition and acceptance within society as trusted experts, and while this has traditionally been the case for doctors and other health professionals, in recent years there has been an increase in complaints against individual practitioners (Allsop, 2006). This has not, however, translated into disillusionment with the medical system per se, which is still largely trusted to solve health problems (Denny, 2009b).

## Guided discovery and diagnosis

Here it will be useful to provide a brief overview of medical education, in order to elicit something of the process by which doctors interpret pain and (perhaps) reach a diagnosis. Within Western post-industrial societies the practice of medicine is a scientific and technical discipline (Waitzkin, 1989). In Chapter 1 it was argued that this was a result of historical, social and technological changes which influenced the construction of medical knowledge. The training of doctors is organised so as to fit them into this model of production. Despite recent changes to medical education (General Medical Council, 2009), medical students continue to be taught clinical skills by a method of guided discovery – the clinical lecturer or consultant will lead the student through a series of questions about a patient which will hopefully guide him or her to the correct diagnosis. Despite the fact that, as Renée Fox argues, 'uncertainty is inherent in medicine' (2000: 409), guided discovery actually generates an illusion of certainty, the implication being that the diagnosis is there waiting to be unveiled as long as the right questions are asked.

In Chapters 3 and 6 we explored the meaning of diagnosis for the patient, but the drive to reach a diagnosis is also extremely strong for clinicians, and it has been argued that diagnostic categorisation is one of the most important professional skills in medicine (Waitzkin, 1989). Diagnosis is important within biomedicine because it sets in train a process of interventions and treatments. Lack of a diagnosis, as we have seen, may lead to ad hoc responses to symptoms and suspicions of malingering or hypochondria.

It is usually doctors who diagnose disease, starting from the patient's narrative on how they perceive their problem; but in listening to this narrative, doctors may interrupt the patient and direct them to concentrate on those aspects which they believe will contribute to a diagnosis. Those parts of the story that are not consistent with informing diagnostic categories will then be excluded from the interaction, even though for the patient they may be very important in providing the context for their complaint. So, for example, a doctor may ask a patient to score his back pain on a scale from zero to ten, whereas the patient may want to differentiate the severity of the pain in relation to different activities. But the doctor only wants one score to record. Waitzkin argues that this makes diagnostic reasoning 'limited and exclusionary' in that it ignores a large part of the patient's experience (1989: 230). In addition, the patient's records will only record the pain score, and not the fact that there was some variation reported in his narrative. For a doctor then, the patient's pain is an aid to diagnosis, and interest in its type and severity may only be relevant as part of a diagnostic classification.

Pain scales that quantify and objectify levels of pain and reduce the complex experience to a single number are more useful to clinicians on their voyage of guided discovery than to patients, who are more focused on the impact the pain is having on their lives. Similarly, following treatment, the clinician will use pain scales to judge the effectiveness of the treatment, whereas the patient may be more interested in how their quality of life has (or has not) been affected. In short, pain scales are linear and unidimensional, whereas the experience of pain is multidimensional. The doctor's focus on the level of pain, while important, excludes its duration and quality, which may be of more importance in the patient's context (Denny, 2009b). This leads to what has been called a clash of perspectives (Freidson, 1970), as the doctor views the patient within the framework of medical knowledge, whereas the patient assesses their illness within their own cultural and social context. This discordance can result in limited communication as well as frustration for both parties, and even in current medical practice, where patients are expected to become more engaged with their healthcare, it is still the doctor who holds jurisdictional authority over diagnosis (Jutel and Nettleton, 2011).

Diagnosis, then, is not an exact science, and indeed it has

often been called an art, although to make a dualistic division such as this may be to oversimplify the reality of the patient–physician encounter. However, as will become clear in the following sections, there is much subjectivity involved in the way pain is perceived and responded to by clinicians.

## Heartsink patients

The term 'heartsink patients' is well known to clinicians and was probably first seen in print in a *BMJ* article by the Nottingham GP Tom O'Dowd. He described them as patients 'who give the doctor and staff a feeling of "heartsink" every time they consult. They evoke an overwhelming mixture of exasperation, defeat, and sometimes plain dislike that causes the heart to sink when they consult' (O'Dowd, 1988: 528). Bestowed by the clinician on a patient, and emanating from the former's experience of the latter, it is a label that patients are often unaware of and do not have the power to challenge by questioning the assumptions that underpin it. O'Dowd describes them as a disparate group, the only common feature being the sinking feeling they cause in the clinician.

What constitutes a heartsink patient? Lower social class, female gender, having a thick folder of medical notes, and psychosomatic illness have all been identified as characteristic features (Denny, 2009a). Experiencing intractable pain, which repeatedly brings the patient back to the doctor in search of some relief, is another common feature. Their symptoms often remain unresolved, leading to frustration for both patient and clinician. The characteristics of clinicians who report higher numbers of heartsink patients include inexperience, higher perceived workload, lower job satisfaction and lack of training in communication skills (Butler and Evans, 1999). A good example of how patients with intractable pain may be judged and labelled can be found in a study by Linda McGowan and colleagues on chronic pelvic pain (CPP) in primary care. CPP is one of a group of problematic illnesses where the label describes what is happening (in this case the experience of pain in the pelvis), rather than being a diagnostic label that explains it. The researchers conducted telephone interviews with seventy-five GPs on their perception, treatment and management of CPP. When asked about the psychological and social characteristics of women with CPP, the GPs used words such as 'depressed', 'introverted' and 'anxious', with one reporting: 'I'm talking anecdotally here, they're usually on the big side, quite overweight, they are usually suffering from other pathologies, they are anxious types, worriers, they can be inadequate and they are not the best copers' (McGowan et al., 1999: 307).

Similarly, in a study on lay and medical views of irritable bowel syndrome (IBS), doctors were found to use two definitions, one 'public' and consistent with the textbooks, the other 'private' and focused on the characteristics that were perceived to be typical of IBS patients: female gender, middle-aged worriers who think a lot about their health and bowels (Dixon-Woods and Critchley, 2000). As Dixon-Woods and Critchley go on to argue, these private views can impact on doctors' behaviour, and indeed some GPs in their study differentiated between 'good patients' who accepted the IBS diagnosis and 'bad patients' who resented the label as well as any suggestion of psychological factors. However, as they also point out, many of the doctors in their sample rejected the notion of a 'typical' IBS patient.

These tensions between doctors and patients invite an examination of the differences in the interpretation of pain that can be observed between the person in pain and their clinician.

## Clinicians' perceptions of levels of pain

We saw in Chapter 6 that many people in pain struggle to be believed. We can now consider this from the other side of the interaction, in relation to the attitudes and values that form clinicians' views about patients and their pain. Clinicians' ideas about the levels of pain that people should experience with certain illnesses, and in certain situations, are based on their values, expectations and prior experience. As May et al. state, 'doctors' interactional behaviours and communication skills are exercised through their own contextual experiences of *types* of patients, *types* of problems, *types* of disposal options' (2004: 153, emphasis in original). For example, following surgery it is expected that a patient will have pain and require analgesia. However, it is anticipated that this requirement will reduce as the wound and the organs that were operated on heal, and clinicians will have expectations, usually based on previous patients and accepted norms, as to how long that should take. So there is also a time limit on certain kinds of pain. People expect childbirth to be painful, but less sympathy is invoked by pain following labour. As with diagnosis, the power to interpret and define pain, and the normal response to it, lies with clinicians, usually doctors. So patients are expected to conform to these norms, which may become quite institutionalised, in that hospital policy on pain relief may be based on them in the absence of clear evidence that supports their use.

Certain types of pain will always be believed, even in the absence of observable 'proof', for example the pain of cancer. Cancer is synonymous in many people's minds with pain, and therefore no further explanation is required. The pain of a broken limb, where an injury is either visible or can be seen on an X-ray, is also believed. Yet other types of pain are treated with suspicion, and may be not taken seriously or may be associated with malingering. Examples of pains that are treated with suspicion include low back pain, menstrual pain and fibromyalgia, which have been addressed from the patient's perspective in Chapter 6. So different types of pain exist in a sort of hierarchy, with some having greater status than others (Denny, 2009b).

What is particular about the pains that attract a low status? Here we can draw on the work of Mike Bury (1991). Some illnesses, particularly long-term ones, are not considered to be of great medical interest either because of the low status of the client group (for example mental illness) or because there is no definitive treatment for them, and so clinicians become frustrated by the lack of therapeutic success. These illnesses, as we have seen, may also be characterised by symptoms that are widespread in the wider population in milder form, so actually knowing when to intervene may be difficult. For example, most people experience low back pain occasionally, so it can be difficult for a clinician to know whether the condition will be self-limiting in time or if there is some underlying pathology. This is compounded where there is no visible 'proof', which can then make legitimation of the patient's condition more difficult. Eccleston and colleagues (1997) also argue that pain is a symptom that requires corroborating evidence. In their study of patient and clinician accounts of chronic pain this lack of corroboration led the clinicians to explain the pain as a result of the patient having lost control, or having managed a lesser pain badly in the past, thereby causing it to exacerbate. The clinicians avoided characterising the patients' pain as being 'all in the head' or imagined, but they did view it as a way of behaving that then exacerbated the patients' problems. A key theme of the accounts was that chronic pain is not amenable to medical treatment, which as we have seen in earlier chapters is what most patients are striving for.

A review of the literature found that healthcare providers respond differently to pain in women and men (Hoffman and Tarzian, 2001). The authors reported that men received more narcotics and women more sedatives following coronary artery bypass graft, suggesting that clinicians viewed women as anxious rather than in pain. They also found that in many instances nurses viewed women as being more tolerant of pain and more likely to report it, which is consistent with the views expressed by lay participants in Bendelow's (2000) study reported in Chapter 5. Another study cited in the review found that physically attractive people were more likely to be thought by health professionals to experience less pain than unattractive people. The authors conclude that the perpetuation of stereotypes by health professionals negatively impacts on the provision of pain treatments (Hoffman and Tarzian, 2001). Åsbring and Närvänen (2003) interviewed twenty-six physicians who had been mentioned by some of the participants in a previous study on the experience of chronic fatigue syndrome (CFS) or fibromyalgia (FM) (see Chapter 6). The physicians (who had had at least one encounter with the patients in the previous study) noted a discrepancy between how the patients with these illnesses presented themselves and behaved, and how they expected sick people to behave. As we saw in the study by Werner and Malterud (2003) discussed in Chapter 6, patients also feel that there are expectations about how they should behave in order to be perceived as credible. The physicians also made moral judgements about patients as being illness-fixated or demanding, and expressed scepticism about the existence of both CFS and FM as disease states. They often characterised the patients as having an 'illness' rather than 'disease', which they deemed as less serious. The authors conclude that it was the combination of the physicians' perceptions of CFS and FM and their impression of the patients that led to their judgements about them.

While a lot of research into clinicians' perspectives on chronic pain has been conducted, one study has explored nurses' approach to post-operative pain management (Dihle et al., 2006). The researchers observed and interviewed nurses on surgical wards in Norway. They found that there was a gap between what the nurses professed to do and what they actually did in practice, which created an obstacle to patients receiving adequate pain relief. The nurses possessed theoretical knowledge, and believed that they were applying it, but they were not always observed to be doing so in their assessment of and response to pain. They reported that they assessed pain by talking to patients, asking them directly if they were in pain, and by observing non-verbal cues. They also reported giving analgesia as prescribed. However, on observation, discrepancies were noted between this ideal and the actual practice, with patients not receiving the optimal treatment.

As noted in Chapter 5, pain in children has been particularly underestimated and poorly managed. A study with healthcare professionals in three different neonatal intensive care units in Canada considered the role of culture and social context in the provision of pain treatment to premature babies. The researchers found that a supportive and collaborative culture facilitated good pain practices, and threats to autonomous decision making and a complex care provision hindered them (Stevens et al., 2011). Respecting individuals (family as well as staff) and including them in decision making, as well as clarity with regard to roles, helped to constitute a supportive culture, whereas low regard for individuals, autocratic decision making and a task-driven culture with hierarchical relationships formed barriers to this. While the present chapter has mainly focused on the characteristics of professions and professionals as influential in the provision of pain management, this study by Stevens et al. highlights the fact that ward/unit culture is also important in shaping the way in which clinicians function.

## Clinicians inflicting pain

So far we have considered the response of clinicians to the person in pain; however, health professionals are in a paradoxical position in that while their role is to relieve pain and suffering, they may have to do so by inflicting pain. As Cecil Helman (2007) reminds us, many procedures for diagnosing or treating illness can cause pain, and we considered one of these, the pain of procedures following burn injuries, in Chapter 4. Inserting a cannula, surgery and physiotherapy will all cause some amount of pain. The justification for clinicians inflicting pain is that it is done to secure longer-term benefits. This is generally accepted by patients, particularly if they are suffering life-threatening conditions, but in some situations long-term pain can be a result of medical intervention, and the more sophisticated interventions become the greater the likelihood of lingering painful consequences.

People with cancer often survive for many years following treatment, but one of the consequences of this may be an experience of pain that severely impacts on quality of life. Long-term pain associated with treatment includes chemotherapy-induced peripheral neuropathy, radiation-induced pain, and hormone-therapy-induced arthralgia. Stokowski cites Dr Judith Paice, Director of the Cancer Pain Programme at Northwest University: 'Our cancer treatments are unfortunately leaving people with significant pain syndromes . . . although they are not new, these pain syndromes are on our radar screens more now than they were a couple of years ago' (2011: 1).

Scarry (1985) argues that any investigation into the nature of pain must include a consideration of the capacity of human beings to inflict pain on each other. At the margins this includes those whose training and raison d'être is to relieve pain and suffering. Health professionals may be involved in inflicting pain by assisting in torture and other inhuman acts, often as part of government-sanctioned programmes. Although such actions are undertaken by very few individuals, instances have been documented over many years. We may question how those participating in such acts reconcile their actions with their professional values and standards.

Hilde Steppe's (1997) research with nurses who worked in Nazi Germany would suggest that the answers lie both in the changing direction of health policy and in the rationale of the nurses themselves. From 1933 there was a paradigm shift in German healthcare, which meant that the individual was valued only for his or her contribution to the whole. If the individual was deemed unfit to contribute, not only did they not deserve care from society, but society had a duty to banish them for the good of the whole. The ideal for women (so long as they were racially pure) was motherhood, and the concept of maternalism was extended to the workplace where

it influenced women's roles. Nursing, with its history of voca-
tion, was ideally suited to this changing health policy. From
her interviews with nurses who had worked under the Nazi
regime, Steppe identified five categories that described their
positions: the enthusiast, the conformist, the obedient, the
persecuted and the resister. The enthusiasts greatly welcomed
the new regime, but they constituted only around 10 per cent
of nurses. The conformists represented the largest group,
who, at least outwardly, came to terms with the regime and
continued their work. They justified their stance with phrases
such as 'I thought I could prevent something worse', or else
considered themselves too powerless to change things. The
obedient group also continued with their work and carried out
the orders given to them. All those who took part in crimes
against humanity out of obedience, including in the extermi-
nation camps and mental institutions, fell into this group. In
carrying out this work they tried to remain 'good' nurses, by
giving an extra pillow, or helping euthanasia victims to drink
the poison. Less is known about the persecuted nurses, or
those who resisted. Many were dismissed, interned, or were
forced to emigrate. Often, Jewish nurses were sent to concen-
tration camps, where they tried to continue to nurse, but few
survived.

In a review of the literature on doctors' involvement in torture, which considered interviews with both torture survivors
and doctors, Sonntag (2008) identified two aspects that fea-
tured in the rationale. The first concerned 'doctors at risk':
those who have a higher risk of being involved in torture due to
their role or workplace. These include doctors in police, prison
and military institutions, who constitute the majority of those
involved. Both democratic and non-democratic regimes make
use of doctors in these institutions, and the structures within
them can turn the orchestration of torture into a norm. The
second aspect, 'dual loyalty', describes the conflict between a
doctor's professional and ethical responsibility to the patient
and their obligation to a third party, for instance an employer

or the state. For around 20 per cent of the people who were tortured there was some form of medical involvement, from assessing the victim's fitness to be tortured to the amputation of body parts that were not medically indicated.

In 2014 the US Senate Select Committee on Intelligence published the executive summary of its previously redacted report on the CIA's detention and interrogation programme. Although some medical personnel did warn about the risk of some of the activities undertaken, the report found that two contract psychologists had developed interrogation techniques based on learned helplessness, and that doctors and nurses were involved in practices such as waterboarding, force feeding and the administration of rectal infusions. The cardiac surgeon and presenter of the 2015 Reith Lectures, Atul Gawande, reflected the view of many clinicians when he tweeted in December 2014: 'The torture could not proceed [without] medical supervision. The medical profession was deeply embedded in this inhumanity. It was doctors who devised the rectal infusions "as a means of behavioural control".' The report demonstrates how medical personnel working in the military and for the CIA were both 'at risk' and also experienced dual loyalties. They were expected to act in ways that conflicted with their professional and ethical standards, which many did, although many more did not.

In a less formal way doctors have also been involved in the practice of female genital mutilation (FGM) (Serour, 2013). As discussed in Chapter 5, although the practice is illegal in many parts of the world it is still widely carried out on women and girls, despite it being irreversible and having no therapeutic value. Although most FGM is performed by traditional healers on young girls, reinfibulation (restitching of the genitalia) is performed by midwives and doctors following childbirth or gynaecological procedures. Increasingly, health professionals are carrying out the original surgery, and girls may be taken to countries where the procedure is commonplace, although this is also illegal in Western Europe. The rationale for medical involvement is that the risk of complications is reduced when FGM or reinfibulation is performed in a clinical environment, and that the procedure has informed consent, but Serour argues that it is usually undertaken as a source of income. The notion of informed consent can also be questioned in societies where a girl only attains adulthood, and becomes marriageable, following FGM, and where there is strong societal pressure on parents to continue the practice. Although the immediate complications may be reduced by the medicalisation of FGM and reinfibulation, longer-term physical and psychological complications mean that the ethical principle of non-maleficence cannot be upheld.

## Summary

The idea that 'Pain is whatever the experiencing person says it is, existing whenever she says it does' (McCaffery, 1983: 14), has become something of a mantra, frequently repeated by clinicians treating those in pain. However, we have seen in this chapter that health professionals do not uncritically accept the patient's interpretation of their pain, and that their own social and professional context colours the judgements they make about how to manage the pain of an individual. Although clinicians go into medical careers in order to relieve pain and suffering, they cannot always do so. This may lead to a sense of failure, which can result in them avoiding or judging the patients in their care. The trust that Western societies place in health professionals, in particular doctors, that they will be able to prolong life and cure diseases, is in many ways unrealistic, although health professionals may encourage high expectations of their services, particularly in fee-paying systems.

This chapter has been concerned with doctors and other healthcare professionals as occupational groups with professed ethical principles and value systems. On occasion, clinicians do not act in accordance with those principles, assisting in torture or female genital mutilation, for financial or other less tangible rewards. These very specific instances do not fall within the mainstream of medical practice, and they are carried out by very few practitioners, but it is clear that in certain situations some people may be persuaded or be willing to act outside of the professional values which they profess to uphold.

# Concluding Thoughts

This volume has explored pain through a sociological lens. It has employed classic theoretical and conceptual texts and also made use of newer sources, some of which do not take an overtly theoretical stance; nevertheless, by utilising interpretive methodology they add to our understanding of pain from the standpoint of those who experience it. These sources give voice to those who have traditionally been unheard, and contribute to sociological knowledge by challenging some of the hegemonic interpretations of pain from biomedicine and psychology. By doing so they allow us to gain insight into the complex world of pain. How we understand pain has implications for the way in which sufferers make sense of it in the context of their lives, and for how others view both the pain and the individual experiencing it. For this reason, Crawford (2009) advocates the reification of pain; in other words, in order to understand pain it needs first to be viewed as concrete or material, rather than as an abstract concept. As sociology is a broad church, gaining insight into pain has also involved encroaching into the overlapping fields of psychology and anthropology.

Although some people have reported positive outcomes from their experience of pain – for example a closer relationship with a partner, or the opportunity to grow and change as a person – it is overwhelmingly viewed in wholly negative terms. The exception to this is where pain can be viewed as productive, as in childbirth. Here the reason for its acceptance is the prospect of a live baby and the knowledge that the pain will end with delivery. Similarly, post-operative pain is endured in the hope of the amelioration of unwanted symptoms.

There have been a number of recurring themes throughout the preceding chapters, and here I will return to those that
contribute most to the role of a sociology of pain, as noted in
the introduction. To summarise, this role is to deconstruct the
rigid objectivity of the biomedical model, which views the sick
body as a faulty machine in need of repair, and to restore pain
to those who actually experience it (Bendelow, 2000). First,
pain is universally experienced but intensely private. No one
can know another's pain unless it is expressed, usually by language but sometimes, particularly in children or those with
intellectual disability, by behaviour. However, the experience of
pain may defy literal expression, and only be communicated by
metaphor or pre-linguistic sounds. Moreover, by making pain
public an individual may incur stigma or find that how they are
viewed within their social world has changed. This brings me
on to the second issue, which is the struggle that many people
experience in having their pain believed, by health professionals and by friends, colleagues and family. This seems to be
particularly the case in instances where no objective confirma-
tion for pain can be found, or where symptoms are widespread
in the wider population, so that the usual self-limiting or easily
dealt with experience becomes the yardstick by which to judge
all cases of the same type of pain. In struggling for legitimation, pain sufferers do not challenge the biomedical model, but
rather attempt to live up to its expectations. This leads us to
the relationship between medical work and the patient experience. Health professionals are influenced by and also help to
construct dominant ways of thinking about pain. Structural
factors such as culture, ethnicity and gender intersect to determine the encounters of clinicians and their patients, which
will be played out within an organisational framework over
which neither party has any meaningful control. It is important, however, to avoid essentialising any one factor, as the
way in which they come together to contribute to experience
is complex and nuanced. Macro structural factors intersect
with micro factors of experience and interpretation, for which

sociology can provide a bridge, encompassing as it does both dimensions.

Health professionals train to cure people and relieve suffering. A shift from the predominance of acute and infectious diseases to that of long-term conditions means that the needs of individuals have altered, but so have many of the resources used to treat them. Many high-tech treatments have been developed, and medicine has had a significant degree of success in helping people to live longer lives. Although these treatments are now ubiquitous, few are curative. They may improve the underlying condition, but they can also result in other symptoms, often pain. Treatments for serious illnesses such as cancer, heart disease and HIV/AIDS may all extend life expectancy, but lower quality of life because of a legacy of pain. The hyperbole around these treatments, particularly in the media but also from the health industry and some clinicians, is of ground-breaking and even miracle cures, but the reality is often survival with some aspect of pain and disability. For many, this is a price worth paying, but as a society we need to accept that there are long-term consequences for individuals, their families, and for the provision of healthcare.

This also begs the question: is the aim of pain relief to reduce or eradicate pain? A dissonance between the responses of the health professional and the patient to this question may lie at the root of conflict between them and help to explain reported dissatisfaction with health service provision. At the heart of this is the idea of pain as contested. There is no single method of treating pain, particularly if the cause is unknown, and individuals may exercise choice in deciding on a healthcare provider, although in the absence of relief the notion of choice needs to be seen as something less than a means of control.

The experience of pain has been communicated in this book for the most part by way of patients' narratives. These have demonstrated the limitation of quantitative measures when it comes to capturing the extent to which pain encroaches on all aspects of life and relationships. They have also, implicitly or explicitly, shown pain to be an embodied experience, as something that an individual has, as well as something that contributes to who they are. The narratives have also allowed us to explore the way in which cultural values have impacted on the experience of pain and on access to health services. For example, the stories from men about wanting or needing to conform to male roles and scripts, and to be stoical and strong in the face of both physical and emotional pain, contributed to an explanation of the reluctance many have to admitting to such pain.

A further theme has been the idea that pain is bounded by uncertainty, which exists at a number of levels. For the person in pain, their pain is certain, something that they know and which they may choose to communicate to others. For those who hear about pain, there is uncertainty, they cannot 'know' it in the same way as the person experiencing it (Scarry, 1985). This uncertainty adds to the problem of legitimation – the lack of a formal diagnostic category or the addition of labels such as 'non-specific' making it difficult for individuals to accept pain, with consequences for how they are able to live their lives. Even with a diagnosis, uncertainty may exist over the illness trajectory or the prognosis. Many of the conditions in which uncertainty is a common factor are not life-threatening, and are of low medical interest; nevertheless, their impact on all aspects of life may be immense.

As was stated in the introduction, sociology is an additional prism though which to view the world of pain. It adds to the hegemonic disciplines of biomedicine and psychology, as well as offering a challenge to them, and unpacks some of the multi-layered facets of the experience of pain. This book has endeavoured to provide an introduction to some of the most relevant concepts from sociology as well as empirical data in order to explore the complex issue of pain.

# References

Aasbø, G., Solbrække, K. N., Kristvik, E. and Werner, A. 2016. Between disruption and continuity: challenges in maintaining the 'biographical we' when caring for a partner with a severe, chronic illness. *Sociology of Health and Illness*, 38, 782–96.

Abrams, P. 1982. *Historical Sociology*. Somerset: Open Books.

Abrams, T. E., Ogletree, R. J., Ratnapradipa, D. and Neumeister, M. W. 2016. Adult survivors' lived experience of burns and post-burn health: a qualitative analysis. *Burns*, 42, 152–62.

Adamson, C. 1997. Existential and clinical uncertainty in the medical encounter: an idiographic account of an illness trajectory defined by inflammatory bowel disease and avascular necrosis. *Sociology of Health and Illness*, 19, 133–59.

Agence France Presse. 2016. Egyptian girl dies during banned female genital mutilation operation. *Guardian*, 31 May, https://www.theguardian.com/world/2016/may/31/egyptian-girl-dies-during-banned-female-genital-mutilation-operation (accessed 31 August 2016).

Ahmad, W. I. U. and Bradby, H. 2007. Locating ethnicity and health: exploring concepts and contexts. *Sociology of Health and Illness*, 29, 795–810.

Allsop, J. 2006. Regaining trust in medicine: professional and state strategies. *Current Sociology*, 54, 621–36.

Amnesty International. 2014. *Torture in 2014: 30 Years of Broken Promises*. Available at www.amnesty.org.uk (accessed 14 September 2016).

Anderson, M. and Asnani, M. 2013. 'You just have to live with it': coping with sickle cell disease in Jamaica. *Qualitative Health Research*, 23, 655–64.

Annandale, E. and Riska, E. 2009. New connections: towards a gender-inclusive approach to women's and men's health. *Current Sociology*, 57, 123–33.

Anon. 2016a. Female genital mutilation: an agonising choice. *The Economist*. Available at www.economist.com (accessed 3 September 2016).

Anon. 2016b. The unkindest cut. *The Economist*. Available at www. economist.com (accessed 3 September 2016).

Armstrong, D. 1994. Bodies of knowledge / knowledge of bodies. In Jones, C. and Porter, R. (eds) *Reassessing Foucault: Power, Medicine and the Body*. Abingdon: Routledge.

Arney, W. R. and Neill, J. 1982. The location of pain in childbirth: natural childbirth and the transformation of obstetrics. *Sociology of Health and Illness*, 4, 1–24.

Arora, K. S. and Jacobs, A. J. 2016. Female genital alteration: a compromise solution. *Journal of Medical Ethics*, 42, 148–54.

Åsbring, P. and Närvänen, A.-L. 2003. Ideal versus reality: physicians' perspectives on patients with chronic fatigue syndrome (CFS) and fibromyalgia. *Social Science and Medicine*, 57, 711–20.

Åsbring, P. and Närvänen, A. 2004. Patient power and control: a study of women with uncertain illness trajectories. *Qualitative Health Research*, 14, 226–40.

Ballard, K., Lawton, K. and Wright, J. 2006. What's the delay? A qualitative study of women's experience of reaching a diagnosis of endometriosis. *Fertility and Sterility*, 5, 1296–301.

Barker, K. K. 2011. Listening to Lyrica: contested illnesses and pharmaceutical determinism. *Social Science and Medicine*, 73, 833–42.

Baszanger, I. 1989. Pain: its experience and treatments. *Social Science and Medicine*, 29, 425–34.

Baszanger, I. 1992. Deciphering chronic pain. *Sociology of Health and Illness*, 14, 181–215.

Baszanger, I. 1998. *Inventing Pain Medicine: From the Laboratory to the Clinic*. New Brunswick: Rutgers University Press.

Bendelow, G. 1993. Pain perceptions, gender and emotion. *Sociology of Health and Illness*, 15, 273–94.

Bendelow, G. A. 1996. A failure of modern medicine? Lay perspectives on a pain relief clinic. In Williams, S. J. and Calnan, M. (eds) *Modern Medicine: Lay Perspectives and Experiences*. London: UCL Press.

Bendelow, G. A. 2000. *Pain and Gender*. Harlow: Prentice Hall.

Bendelow, G. A. 2009. *Health, Emotion and the Body*. Cambridge: Polity.

Bendelow, G. A. and Williams, S. J. 1996. The end of the road? Lay views on a pain-relief clinic. *Social Science and Medicine*, 43, 1127–36.

Bendelow, G. A. and Williams, S. J. 2002. Natural for women: abnormal for men. Beliefs about pain and gender. In Nettleton S. and Watson, J. (eds) *The Body in Everyday Life*. London: Routledge.

Bissonette, J. M. 2008. Adherence: a concept analysis. *Journal of Advanced Nursing*, 63, 634–43.

Black, C. and Rowling, E. 2009. Assessing complementary practice: building consensus on appropriate research methods. Report of an Independent Advisory Group, London, King's Fund.

Blaxter, M. 2009. The case of the vanishing patient? Illness and experience. *Sociology of Health and Illness*, 31, 762–78.

Blumer, H. 1969. *Symbolic Interactionism: Perspective and Method.* Englewood Cliffs: Prentice Hall.

Bogle, V. undated. No frills. Qualitative research into men, health, the internet and Man MOT. Available at https://www.menshealthforum. org.uk/sites/default/files/pdf/haringey_man_mot_no_frills_for_ publication.pdf (accessed 26 January 2017).

Bradby, H. 2012. *Medicine, Health and Society.* London: Sage.

Bridges, S. 2012. Chronic pain. In Craig, R. and Mindell, J. (eds) *Health Survey for England,* Volume 1. London: The Health and Social Care Information Centre.

Britten, N. 2001. Prescribing and the defence of clinical autonomy. *Sociology of Health and Illness*, 23, 478–96.

Brown, G. W. and Harris, T. O. 1978. *The Social Origins of Depression.* London: Tavistock.

Bury, M. 1982. Chronic illness as biographical disruption. *Sociology of Health and Illness*, 4, 167–82.

Bury, M. 1991. The sociology of chronic illness: a review of research and prospects. *Sociology of Health and Illness*, 13, 451–68.

Bury, M. 1997. *Health and Illness in a Changing Society.* London: Routledge.

Bury, M. 2001. Illness narrative: fact or fiction. *Sociology of Health and Illness*, 23, 263–85.

Butler, C. C. and Evans, M. 1999. The 'heartsink' patient revisited. *British Journal of General Practice*, 49, 230–3.

Calpin, P., Imran, A. and Harmon, D. 2016. A comparison of expectations of physicians and patients with chronic pain for pain clinic visits. *Pain Practice.* Available at http://onlinelibrary.wiley.com/ doi/10.1111/papr.12428/full (accessed 10 May 2017).

Carter, B., McArthur, E. and Cunliffe, M. 2002. Dealing with uncertainty: parental assessment of pain in their children with profound special needs. *Journal of Advanced Nursing*, 38, 449–57.

Chan, M. Y. P., Hamamura, T. and Janschewitz, K. 2013. Ethnic differences in physical pain sensitivity: role of acculturation. *Pain*, 154, 119–23.

Charmaz, K. 2010. Disclosing illness and disability in the workplace. *Journal of International Education in Business*, 3, 6–19.

Clark, D. 1999. 'Total pain': disciplinary power and the body in the work of Cicely Saunders, 1958–1967. *Social Science and Medicine*, 49, 727–36.

Clarke, K. A. and Iphofen, R. 2005. Believing the patient with chronic pain: a review of the literature. *British Journal of Nursing*, 14, 490–3.

Cline, R. J. W., Harper, F. W. K., Penner, L. A., Peterson, A. M., Taub, J. W. and Albrecht, T. L. 2006. Parent communication and child pain and distress during painful pediatric cancer treatments. *Social Science and Medicine* (1982), 63, 883–98.

Coleman, B., Ellis-Caird, H., McGowan, J. and Benjamin, M. J. 2016. How sickle cell disease patients experience, understand and explain their pain: an interpretative phenomenological analysis study. *British Journal of Health Psychology*, 21, 190–203.

Comte, A. 1975. *Auguste Comte and Positivism: The Essential Writings*, ed. Lenzer, G. New Jersey: Transaction Publishers.

Corbett, M., Foster, N. E. and Ong, B. N. 2007. Living with low back pain: stories of hope and despair. *Social Science and Medicine*, 65, 1584–94.

Cornwell, J. 1984. *Hard Earned Lives*. London: Tavistock.

Courtenay, W. H. 2000. Constructions of masculinity and their influence on men's well-being: a theory of gender and health. *Social Science and Medicine*, 50, 1385–401.

Cox, H., Henderson, L., Wood, R. and Cagliarini, G. 2003. Learning to take charge: women's experiences of living with endometriosis. *Complementary Therapies in Nursing and Midwifery*, 9, 62–8.

Crawford, C. S. 2009. From pleasure to pain: the role of the MPQ in the language of phantom limb pain. *Social Science and Medicine*, 69, 655–61.

Crow, L. 1996. Including all of our lives: renewing the social model of disability. In Barnes, C. and Mercer, G. (eds) *Exploring the Divide: Illness and Disability*. Leeds: Disability Press.

Culley, L., Hudson, N. and Lohan, M. 2013. Where are all the men? The marginalization of men in social scientific research on infertility. *Reproductive Biomedicine Online*, 27, 225–35.

Culley, L., Hudson, N., Mitchell, H., Law, C., Denny, E. and Raine-Fenning, N. 2013a. Endometriosis: improving the wellbeing of couples. Summary report and recommendations. Available at www.dmu.ac.uk/endopartreport (accessed 4 March 2017).

Culley, L., Hudson, N., Law, C., Denny, E., Mitchell, H., Baumgarten, M. and Raine-Fenning, N. 2013b. The social and psychological impact of endometriosis on women's lives: a critical narrative review. *Human Reproduction Update*, 19, 625–39.

Da Mota Gomes, M. and Engelhardt, E. 2014. A neurological bias in the history of hysteria: from the womb to the nervous system and Charcot. *Archivos de Neuro-Psiquiatria*, 72, 972–5.

Denny, E. 1993. The experience of in vitro fertilization and gamete intra-fallopian transfer. *Journal of Advanced Nursing*, 18, 511–17.

Denny, E. 2004a. Women's experience of endometriosis. *Journal of Advanced Nursing*, 46, 641–8.

Denny, E. 2009a. 'I never know from one day to another how I will feel': pain and uncertainty in women with endometriosis. *Qualitative Health Research*, 19, 985–95.

Denny, E. 2004b. 'You are one of the unlucky ones': delay in the diagnosis of endometriosis. *Diversity in Health and Social Care*, 1, 39–44.

Denny, E. 2009b. Heartsink patients and intractable conditions. In Denny, E. and Earle, S. (eds) *The Sociology of Long Term Conditions and Nursing Practice*. Basingstoke: Palgrave Macmillan.

Denny, E. 2010. Experiencing and managing medically unexplained conditions: the case of chronic pelvic pain in women. In Lloyd, C. and Heller, T. (eds) *Long-Term Conditions: Challenges in Health and Social Care Practice*. London: Sage.

Denny, E. 2015. Long term conditions and disability. In Deery, R., Denny, E. and Letherby, G. (eds) *Sociology for Midwives*. Cambridge: Polity.

Denny, E. and Mann, C. H. 2008. Endometriosis and the primary care consultation. *European Journal of Obstetrics, Gynecology, and Reproductive Biology*, 139, 111–15.

Dihle, A., Bjølseth, G. and Helseth, S. 2006. The gap between saying and doing in postoperative pain management. *Journal of Clinical Nursing*, 15, 469–79.

Dixon-Woods, M. and Critchley, S. 2000. Medical and lay views of irritable bowel syndrome. *Family Practice*, 17, 108–13.

Donovan, J. L. and Blake, R. 1992. Patient non-compliance: deviance or reasoned decision making? *Social Science and Medicine*, 34, 507–13.

Dunham, M., Ingleton, C., Ryan, T. and Gott, M. 2013. A narrative literature review of older people's cancer pain experience. *Journal of Clinical Nursing*, 22, 2100–13.

Durkheim, E. 1952. *Suicide: A Study in Sociology*. London: Routledge and Kegan Paul.

Eaves, E. R., Sherman, K. J., Ritenbaugh, C., Hsu, C., Nichter, M., Turner, J. A. and Cherkin, D. C. 2015. A qualitative study of changes in expectations over time among patients with chronic low back pain seeking four CAM therapies. *BMC Complementary and Alternative Medicine*, 15, 12.

Eccleston, C., Williams, A. C. and Stainton-Rogers, W. 1997. Patients' and professionals' understandings of the causes of chronic pain: blame, responsibility and identity protection. *Social Science and Medicine*, 45, 699–709.

Ellis, H. 2010. The early days of anaesthesia. *Journal of Perioperative Practice*, 20, 302–3.

Ellis, J., Cobb, M., O'Connor, T., Dunn, L., Irving, G. and Lloyd-Williams, M. 2015. The meaning of suffering in patients with advanced progressive cancer. *Chronic Illness*, 11, 198–209.

Engel, G. L. 1977. The need for a new medical model. *Science*, 196, 129–36.

Eriksson, K., Wikström, L., Årestedt, K., Fridlund, B. and Broström, A. 2014. Numeric rating scale: patients' perceptions of its use in postoperative pain assessments. *Applied Nursing Research*, 27, 41–6.

Eriksson, M. and Svedlund, M. 2006. 'The intruder': spouses' narratives about life with a chronically ill partner. *Journal of Clinical Nursing*, 15, 324–33.

Ersek, M., Kraybill, E. M. and Du Penn, A. 1999. Factors hindering patients' use of medications for cancer pain. *Cancer Practice*, 7, 226–32.

Esfahlan, A. J., Lotfi, M., Zamanzadeh, V. and Babaduor, J. 2010. Burn pain and patients' responses. *Burns*, 36, 1129–33.

Exley, C. and Letherby, G. 2001. Managing a disrupted lifecourse: issues of identity and emotion work. *Health: An Interdisciplinary Journal for the Social Study of Health, Illness and Medicine*, 5, 112–32.

Fayaz, A., Croft, P., Langford, R., Donaldson, L. and Jones, G. 2016. Prevalence of chronic pain in the UK: a systematic review and meta-analysis of population studies. *BMJ Open*, 6, e010364.

Findlay, L., Williams, A. C. de C. and Scior, K. 2014. Exploring experiences and understandings of pain in adults with intellectual disabilities. *Journal of Intellectual Disability Research*, 58, 358–67.

Finnstrom, B. and Soderhamn, O. 2006. Conceptions of pain among Somali women. *Journal of Advanced Nursing*, 54, 418–25.

Foucault, M. 1973. *The Birth of the Clinic: An Archaeology of Medical Perception*. London: Tavistock.

Fox, R. C. 2000. Medical uncertainty revisited. In Albrecht, G. L., Fitzpatrick, R. and Scrimshaw, S. C. (eds) *The Handbook of Social Studies in Health and Medicine*. London: Sage.

Francis, L. and Fitzpatrick, J. J. 2012. Post-operative pain: nurses' knowledge and patients' experiences. *Pain Management Nursing*, 14, 351–7.

Frank, A. W. 1990. Bringing bodies back in: a decade review. *Theory, Culture and Society*, 7, 131–62.

Frank, A. W. 1991. *At the Will of the Body: Reflections on Illness.* Boston: Houghton-Mifflin.

Frank, A. W. 1995. *The Wounded Storyteller: Body, Illness and Ethics.* Chicago: University of Chicago Press.

Frank, A. W. 2000. The standpoint of storyteller. *Qualitative Health Research*, 10, 354–65.

Frank, A. W. 2001. Can we research suffering? *Qualitative Health Research*, 11, 353–62.

Frank, A. W. 2005. Generosity, care and a narrative interest in pain. In Carr, D. B., Loeser, J. D. and Morris, D. B. (eds) *Narrative, Pain and Suffering.* Seattle: IASP Press.

Freidson, E. 1970. *Profession of Medicine.* Chicago: University of Chicago Press.

Freund, P. E. 1990. The expressive body: a common ground for the sociology of emotions and health and illness. *Sociology of Health and Illness*, 12, 452–77.

Gan, T. J., Habib, A. S., Miller, T. E., White, W. and Apfelbaum, J. L. 2014. Incidence, patient satisfaction, and perceptions of post-surgical pain: results from a US national survey. *Current Medical Research and Opinion*, 30, 149–60.

Gatchel, R. J. 2013. The biopsychosocial model of chronic pain. *Clinical Insights: Chronic Pain*, 5, 5–17.

Gatchel, R. J. and Maddrey, A. M. 2004. The biopsychosocial perspective of pain. In Raczynski, J. M. and Leviton, L. C. (eds) *Handbook of Clinical Health Psychology: Volume 2. Disorders of Behavior and Health.* Washington, DC: American Psychological Association.

General Medical Council. 2009. Tomorrow's doctors. Available at http://www.gmc-uk.org/education/undergraduate/tomorrows_doctors_2009_standards.asp (accessed 15 August 2013).

Ghaemi, S. N. 2011. The biopsychosocial model in psychiatry: a critique. *Existenz*, 6, 1–8.

Giddens, A. 1971. *Capitalism and Modern Social Theory: An Analysis of the Writings of Marx, Durkheim and Max Weber.* Cambridge: Cambridge University Press.

Glenton, C. 2003. Chronic back pain sufferers: striving for the sick role. *Social Science and Medicine*, 57, 2243–52.

Goffman, E. 1968. *Stigma: Notes on the Management of a Spoiled Identity.* Harmondsworth: Penguin.

Goudsmit, E. M. 1994. All in her mind! Stereotypic views and the psychologisation of women's illness. In Wilkinson, S. and Kitzinger, C. (eds) *Women and Health.* London: Taylor and Francis.

Goyal, M. K., Kuppermann, N., Cleary, S. D., Teach, S. J. and

Chamberlain, J. M. 2015. Racial disparities in pain management of children with appendicitis in emergency departments. *JAMA Pediatrics*, 169, 996–1002.

Grace, V. 2003. Embodiment and meaning: understanding chronic pelvic pain. *Journal of Consciousness Studies*, 10, 41–60.

Grace, V. and MacBride-Stewart, S. 2007. 'Women get this': gendered meanings of chronic pelvic pain. *Health: An Interdisciplinary Journal for Social Study of Health, Illness and Medicine*, 11, 47–67.

Grace, V. and Zondervan, K. 2006. Chronic pelvic pain in women in New Zealand: comparative wellbeing, co-morbidity, and impact on work and other activities. *Health Care for Women International*, 27, 585–99.

Hall, H., Brosnan, C. and Collins, M. 2017. Nurses' attitudes towards complementary therapies: a systematic review and meta-synthesis. *International Journal of Nursing Studies*, 69, 47–66.

Haoussou, K. 2016. When your patient is a survivor of torture. *BMJ*. Available at BMJ 2016;355:i1509 (accessed 15 November 2016).

Harrison, A. 2003. Getting the right medicines. King's Fund. Available at www.kingsfund.org.uk/publications (accessed 21 January 2017).

Hawthorne, J. 2007. Cartesian dualism. In van Inwagen, P. and Zimmerman, D. (eds) *Persons Human and Divine*. Oxford: The Clarendon Press.

Helman, C. G. 2007. *Culture, Health and Illness*, 5th edition. London: Hodder Arnold.

Hemlow, J. (ed.) 1975. *The Journals and Letters of Fanny Burney (Madame D'Arblay)*. Oxford: The Clarendon Press.

Hinton, L. and Miller, T. 2013. Mapping men's anticipations and experiences in the reproductive realm: (in)fertility journeys. *Reproductive BioMedicine Online*, 27, 244–52.

Hoffman, D. E. and Tarzian, A. J. 2001. The girl who cried pain: a bias against women in the treatment of pain. *Journal of Law, Medicine and Ethics*, 29, 13–27.

Hoffman, K. M., Trawalter, S., Axt, J. R. and Oliver, M. N. 2016. Racial bias in pain assessment and treatment recommendations, and false beliefs about biological differences between blacks and whites. *Proceedings of the National Academy of Sciences*, 113, 4296–301.

HSCIC. 2016. First ever annual statistical publication for FGM shows 5,700 newly recorded cases during 2015–16. NHS digital. Available at www.digital.nhs.uk (accessed 31 August 2016).

Hudson, N. and Culley, L. 2015. Infertility and assisted conception. In Deery, R., Denny, E. and Letherby, G. (eds) *Sociology for Midwives*. Cambridge: Polity.

Hudson, N., Culley, L., Law, C., Mitchell, H. and Denny, E. 2013. Conducting dyadic research in chronic illness: men, women, and endometriosis. Paper presented to the British Sociological Association Medical Sociology Annual Conference, University of York, 11–13 September.

Hudson, N., Culley, L., Law, C., Mitchell, H., Denny, E. and Raine-Fenning, N. 2016. 'We needed to change the mission statement of the marriage': biographical disruptions, appraisals and revisions among couples living with endometriosis. *Sociology of Health and Illness*, 38, 721–35.

Hughes, B. and Paterson, K. 1997. The social model of disability and the disappearing body: towards a sociology of impairment. *Disability and Society*, 12, 325–40.

Huntington, A. and Gilmour, J. A. 2005. A life shaped by pain: women and endometriosis. *Journal of Clinical Nursing*, 14, 1124–32.

Hydén, L. C. 1997. Illness and narrative. *Sociology of Health and Illness*, 19, 48–69.

James, N. and Field, D. 1992. The routinization of hospice: charisma and bureaucratization. *Social Science and Medicine*, 34, 1363–75.

Jarrett, N., Payne, S., Turner, P. and Hillier, R. 1999. 'Someone to talk to' and 'pain control': what people expect from a specialist palliative care team. *Palliative Medicine*, 13, 139–44.

Jenkins, L. 2015. Negotiating pain: the joint construction of a child's bodily sensation. *Sociology of Health and Illness*, 37, 298–311.

Jewson, N. D. 1976. The disappearance of the sick-man from medical cosmology, 1770–1870. *Sociology*, 10, 225–44.

Jobling, R. 1988. The experience of psoriasis under treatment. In Anderson, R. and Bury, M. (eds) *Living with Chronic Illness: The Experience of Patients and their Families*. London: Unwin Hyman.

Johnson, J. E. and Johnson, K. E. 2006. Ambiguous chronic illness in women: a community health nursing concern. *Journal of Community Health Nursing*, 23, 159–67.

Jones, G. L., Jenkinson, C. and Kennedy, S. 2004. The impact of endometriosis on quality of life: a qualitative analysis. *Journal of Psychosomatic Obstetrics and Gynecology*, 2, 123–33.

Jutel, A. and Nettleton, S. 2011. Towards a sociology of diagnosis: reflections and opportunities. *Social Science and Medicine*, 73, 793–800.

Karasz, A. and Anderson, M. 2003. The vaginitis monologues: women's experiences of vaginal complaints in a primary care setting. *Social Science and Medicine*, 56, 1013–21.

Kavalieratos, D., Mitchell, E. M., Carey, T. S., Dev, S., Biddle, A. K., Reeve, B. B., Abernethy, A. P. and Weinberger, M. 2014. 'Not the "grim reaper service"': an assessment of provider knowledge, attitudes, and perceptions regarding palliative care referral barriers in heart failure. *Journal of the American Heart Association*, 3, e000544.

Kelly, B. 2016. We need better data on FGM not propaganda. *Guardian*, 31 July.

Kessler, R. C. and Bromet, E. J. 2013. The epidemiology of depression across cultures. *Annual Review of Public Health*, 34, 119–38.

Kleinman, A. 1988. *The Illness Narratives: Suffering, Healing and the Human Condition*. New York: Basic Books.

Kleinman, A. and Seeman, D. 2000. Personal experience of illness. In Albrecht G. L., Fitzpatrick, R. and Scrimshaw, S. C. (eds) *Handbook of Social Studies in Health and Medicine*. London: Sage.

Labuski, C. 2015. *It Hurts Down There: The Bodily Imaginaries of Female Genital Pain*. New York: SUNY Press.

Larsson, A. T. and Grassman, E. J. 2012. Bodily changes among people living with physical impairments and chronic illnesses: biographical disruption or normal illness? *Sociology of Health and Illness*, 34, 1156–69.

Lasch, K. E. 2005. Putting pain and suffering in their place. In Carr, D. B., Loeser, J. D. and Morris, D. B. (eds) *Narrative, Pain and Suffering*. Seattle: IASP Press.

Lee, C. 2009. 'Race' and 'ethnicity' in biomedical research: how do scientists construct and explain differences in health? *Social Science and Medicine*, 68, 1183–90.

Letherby, G. 1999. Other than mother and mothers as others: the experience of motherhood and non-motherhood in relation to 'infertility' and 'involuntary childlessness'. *Women's Studies International Forum*, 22, 359–72.

Lewis, C. S. 1940. *The Problem of Pain*. London: The Centenary Press.

Locock, L. and Ziébland, S. 2015. Mike Bury: biographical disruption and long-term and other health conditions. In Collyer, F. (ed) *The Palgrave Handbook of Social Theory in Health, Illness and Medicine*. Basingstoke: Palgrave Macmillan.

Longard, J., Twycross, A., Williams, A. M., Hong, P. and Chorney, J. 2016. Parents' experiences of managing their child's postoperative pain at home: an exploratory qualitative study. *Journal of Clinical Nursing*, 25, 2619–28.

Lundborg, C. 2015. Why postoperative pain remains a problem. *Journal of Pain and Palliative Care Pharmacotherapy*, 29, 300–2.

Lynch, C. 2015. *The C Word*. London: Random House.

McCaffery, M. 1983. *Nursing the Patient in Pain*. London: Harper and Row.

McCann, H. J. 2012. Divine Providence. *Stanford Encyclopedia of Philosophy*. Available at http://plato.stanford.edu/archives/win2012/entries/providence-divine (accessed 10 May 2017).

McCluskey, S., De Vries, H., Reneman, M., Brooks, J. and Brouwer, S. 2015. 'I think positivity breeds positivity': a qualitative exploration of the role of family members in supporting those with chronic musculoskeletal pain to stay at work. *BMC Family Practice*, 16, 85.

Macfarlane, A. J. and Dorkenoo, E. 2015. Prevalence of female mutilation in England and Wales: national and local estimates. London: City University in association with Equality Now.

McGarry, J., Simpson, C. and Mansour, M. 2010. How domestic abuse affects the wellbeing of older women. *Nursing Older People*, 22, 33–7.

McGowan, L., Escott, D., Luker, K., Creed, F. and Chew-Graham, C. 2010. Is chronic pelvic pain a comfortable diagnosis for primary care practitioners: a qualitative study. Available at http://www.biomedcentral.com/1471–2296/11/7 (accessed 26 June 2016).

McGowan, L., Luker, K., Creed, F. and Chew-Graham, C. A. 2007. 'How do you explain a pain that can't be seen?': the narratives of women with chronic pelvic pain and their disengagement with the diagnostic cycle. *British Journal of Health Psychology*, 12, 261–74.

McGowan, L., Pitts, M. and Carter, D. C. 1999. Chronic pelvic pain: the General Practitioners' perspective. *Psychology, Health and Medicine*, 4, 303–17.

Maciver, D., Jones, D. and Nicol, M. 2010. Parents' experiences of caring for a child with chronic pain. *Qualitative Health Research*, 20, 1272–82.

McKenry, P. C., Serovich, J. M., Mason, T. L. and Mosack, K. 2006. Perpetration of gay and lesbian partner violence: a disempowerment perspective. *Journal of Family Violence*, 21, 233–43.

McKinley, J. B. 1977. The business of good doctoring or doctoring as good business: reflections of Friedson's views on the medical game. *International Journal of Health Services*, 7, 459–83.

Manias, E. 2012. Complexities of pain assessment and management in hospitalised older people: a qualitative observation and interview study. *International Journal of Nursing Studies*, 49, 1243–54.

Marcovic, M., Manderson, L. and Warren, N. 2008. Endurance and contest: women's narratives of endometriosis. *Health: An Interdisciplinary Journal for Social Study of Health, Illness and Medicine*, 12, 349–67.

Marsh, I., Keating, M., Punch, S. and Harden, J. 2009. *Sociology: Making Sense of Society*, 4th edition. Harlow: Pearson Longman.

Martins, J. T., Bobroff, M., Ribiero, R. P., Soares, M. H., Robazzi, M. and Marziale, M. 2014. Feelings experienced by the nursing team at a burns treatment center. *Escola Anna Nery*, 18, 522–6.

May, C., Allison, G., Chapple, A., Chew-Graham, C., Dixon, C., Gask, L., Graham, R., Rogers, A. and Roland, M. 2004. Framing the doctor-patient relationship in chronic illness: a comparative study of general practitioners' accounts. *Sociology of Health and Illness*, 26, 135–58.

Melzack, R. 2001. Pain and the neuromatrix in the brain. *Journal of Dental Education*, 65, 1378–82.

Melzack, R. and Wall, P. D. 1965. Pain mechanisms: a new theory. *Science*, 150, 971–9.

Melzack, R. and Wall, P. D. 1968. Gate control theory of pain. In Soulairoc, A., Cahn, J. and Charpentier, J. (eds) *Pain*. New York: Academic Press.

Mills, C. W. 1970. *The Sociological Imagination*. Harmondsworth: Penguin.

Morris, B. J., Krieger, J. N. and Klausner, D. 2016. Critical evaluation of unscientific arguments disparaging affirmative infant male circumcision policy. *World Journal of Clinical Pediatrics*, 5, 251–61.

Nagy, S. 1999. Strategies used by burns nurses to cope with the infliction of pain on patients. *Journal of Advanced Nursing*, 29, 1427–33.

Nahin, R. L. 2015. Estimates of pain prevalence and severity in adults: United States 2012. *The Journal of Pain*, 16, 769–80.

Navarro, V. 1981. *Imperialism, Health and Medicine*. Farmingdale: Baywood.

Navarro, V. (ed.) 2004. *The Political and Social Contexts of Health*. Farmingdale: Baywood.

Nettleton, S. 1989. Power and pain: the location of pain and fear in dentistry and the creation of a dental subject. *Social Science and Medicine*, 29, 1183–90.

Nettleton, S. 2006a. *The Sociology of Health and Illness*, 2nd edition. Cambridge: Polity.

Nettleton, S. 2006b. 'I just want permission to be ill': towards a sociology of medically unexplained symptoms. *Social Science and Medicine*, 62, 1167–78.

Nettleton, S. 2006c. Understanding the narratives of people who live with unexplained illness. *Patient Education and Counselling*, 56, 205–10.

Newton, B. J., Southall, J. L., Raphael, J. H., Ashford, R. L. and

Lemarchand, K. 2013. A narrative review of the impact of disbelief in chronic pain. *Pain Management Nursing*, 14, 161–71.

Newton, H. 2011. 'Very sore nights and days': the child's experience of illness in early modern England, c.1580–1720. *Medical History*, 55, 153–82.

O'Dowd, T. C. 1988. Five years of heartsink patients in general practice. *British Medical Journal*, 297, 528–30.

Ogunsiji, O., Wilkes, L., Jackson, D. and Peters, K. 2012. Suffering and smiling: West African immigrant women's experience of intimate partner violence. *Journal of Clinical Nursing*, 21, 1659–65.

Oliver, M. and Barnes, C. 2012. *The New Politics of Disablement*. Basingstoke: Palgrave Macmillan.

Palmer, B., Macfarlane, G., Afzal, C., Esmail, A., Silman, A. and Lunt, M. 2007. Acculturation and the prevalence of pain amongst South Asian minority ethnic groups in the UK. *Rheumatology*, 46, 1009–14.

Parkin, F. 1974. Strategies of social closure in class formation. In Parkin, F. (ed.) *The Social Analysis of Class Structure*. London: Tavistock.

Parsons, T. 1951. *The Social System*. London: Routledge and Kegan Paul.

Platts-Mills, T. F., Esserman, D. A., Brown, D. L., Bortsov, A. V., Sloane, P. D. and McLean, S. A. 2012. Older US emergency department patients are less likely to receive pain medication than younger patients: results from a national survey. *Annals of Emergency Medicine*, 60, 199–206.

Playle, J. F. and Keeley, P. 1998. Non-compliance and professional power. *Journal of Advanced Nursing*, 27, 304–11.

Plummer, K. 1996. Symbolic interactionism in the twentieth century: the rise of empirical social theory. In Turner, B. (ed.) *The Blackwell Companion to Social Theory*. Oxford: Blackwell.

Pollak, T. 2013. Hysteria, hysterectomy, and anti-NMDA receptor encephalitis: a modern perspective on an infamous chapter in medicine. *BMJ*, 346, f3756.

Porter, R. 1997. *The Greatest Benefit to Mankind: A Medical History of Humanity from Antiquity to the Present*. London: HarperCollins.

Porter, R. 2000. *Enlightenment: Britain and the Creation of the Modern World*. London: Penguin Books.

Porter, R. and Porter, D. 1988. *In Sickness and in Health*. London: Fourth Estate.

Pound, P., Britten, N., Morgan, M., Yardley, L., Pope, C., Daker-White, G. and Campbell, R. 2005. Resisting medicines: a synthesis of qualitative studies of medicine taking. *Social Science and Medicine*, 61, 133–55.

Rabinow, P. E. 1991. *The Foucault Reader: An Introduction to Foucault's Thought*. London: Penguin.

Radley, A. 2005. Illness narrative and the 'making present' of suffering. In Carr, D. B., Loeser, J. D. and Morris, D. B. (eds) *Narrative, Pain and Suffering*. Seattle: IASP Press.

Rafferty, A. M. 1995. The anomaly of autonomy: space and status in early Victorian reform. *International History of Nursing Journal*, 1, 43–56.

Råheim, M. and Håland, W. 2006. Lived experience of chronic pain and fibromyalgia: women's stories of daily life. *Qualitative Health Research*, 16, 741–61.

Rajan, L. 1996. Pain and pain relief in labour: issues of control. In Williams, S. J. and Calnan, M. (eds) *Modern Medicine: Lay Perspectives and Experiences*. London: UCL Press.

Rey, R. 1995. *The History of Pain*. Cambridge: Harvard University Press.

Rhodes, L. A., McPhillips-Tangum, C. A., Markham, C. and Klenk, R. 2002. The power of the visible: the meaning of diagnostic tests in chronic back pain. In Nettleton, S. and Gustafsson, U. (eds) *The Sociology of Health and Illness Reader*. Cambridge: Polity.

Richardson, J. C. 2005. Establishing the (extra)ordinary in widespread chronic pain. *Health: An Interdisciplinary Journal for Social Study of Health, Illness and Medicine*, 9, 35–48.

Richardson, J. C., Ong, B. N. and Sim, J. 2006. Is chronic widespread pain biographically disruptive? *Social Science and Medicine*, 63, 1573–85.

Risør, M. B. 2009. Illness explanations among patients with medically unexplained symptoms: different idioms for different contexts. *Health: An Interdisciplinary Journal for Social Study of Health, Illness and Medicine*, 13, 505–21.

Robertson, S., Bagnall, A. and Walker, M. 2015. Evidence for a gender-based approach to mental health programmes: identifying the key considerations associated with 'being male'. Available at http://eprints.leedsbeckett.ac.uk (accessed 21 March 2017).

Robinson, I. 1988. *Multiple Sclerosis*. London: Routledge.

Robinson-Papp, J., George, M. C., Dorfman, D. and Simpson, D. M. 2015. Barriers to chronic pain measurement: a qualitative study of patient perspectives. *Pain Medicine*, 16, 1256–64.

Rogers, A. and Pilgrim, D. 2010. *A Sociology of Mental Health and Illness*: London: McGraw-Hill Education.

Rosenberg, C. E. 2002. The tyranny of diagnosis: specific entities and individual experience. *The Millbank Quarterly*, 80, 237–60.

Roth, J. A. 1963. *Timetables*. New York: Bobbs-Merrill.

Rowland, C., Hanratty, B., Pilling, M., van den Berg, B. and Grande, G. 2017. The contributions of family care-givers at end of life: a national post-bereavement census survey of cancer carers' hours of care and expenditures. *Palliative Medicine*, 31, 346–55.

Russell, S., Daly, J., Hughes, E. and op't Hoog, C. 2003. Nurses and 'difficult' patients: negotiating non-compliance. *Journal of Advanced Nursing*, 43, 281–7.

Saarnio, L., Arman, M. and Ekstrand, P. 2012. Power relations in patients' experiences of suffering during treatment for cancer. *Journal of Advanced Nursing*, 68, 271–9.

Sabaté, E. 2003. *Adherence to Long-term Therapies: Evidence for Action.* Geneva: World Health Organization.

Saks, M. 1995. *Professions and the Public Interest: Medical Power, Altruism and Alternative Medicine.* London: Routledge.

Saks, M. 1998. Medicine and complementary medicine. In Scambler, G. and Higgs, P. (eds) *Modernity, Medicine and Health.* London: Routledge.

Samaritans. 2016. *Suicide Statistics Report 2016.* Available at www.samaritans.org (accessed 21 March 2017).

Sanders, C., Donovan, J. and Dieppe, P. 2002. The significance and consequences of having painful and disabled joints in older age: co-existing accounts of normal and disrupted biographies. *Sociology of Health and Illness*, 24, 227–53.

Scambler, G. and Hopkins, A. 1986. 'Being epileptic': coming to terms with stigma. *Sociology of Health and Illness*, 8, 26–43.

Scarry, E. 1985. *The Body in Pain. The Making and Unmaking of the World.* New York: Oxford University Press.

Schafer, L. M., Hsu, C., Eaves, E. R., Ritenbaugh, C., Turner, J., Cherkin, D. C., Sims, C. and Sherman, K. J. 2012. Complementary and alternative medicine (CAM) providers' views of chronic low back pain patients' expectations of CAM therapies: a qualitative study. *BMC Complementary and Alternative Medicine*, 12, 234.

Schaller, A., Larsson, B., Lindblad, M. and Liedberg, G. M. 2015. Experiences of pain: a longitudinal, qualitative study of patients with head and neck cancer recently treated with radiotherapy. *Pain Management Nursing*, 16, 336–45.

Schumacher, K. L., West, C., Dodd, M., Paul, S. M., Tripathy, D., Koo, P. and Miaskowski, C. A. 2002. Pain management autobiographies and reluctance to use opioids for cancer pain management. *Cancer Nursing*, 25, 125–33.

Seear, K. 2009. The etiquette of endometriosis: stigmatisation, menstrual concealment and the diagnostic delay. *Social Science and Medicine*, 69, 1220–7.

Serour, G. I. 2013. Medicalization of female genital mutilation/cutting. *African Journal of Urology*, 19, 145–9.

Shakespeare, T. 2006. *Disability Rights and Wrongs*. London: Routledge.

Sharma, U. 1996. Using complementary therapies: a challenge to orthodox medicine. In Williams, S. J. and Calnan, M. (eds) *Modern Medicine: Lay Perspectives and Experiences*. London: UCL Press.

Sharpe, M. 2001. Medically unexplained symptoms and syndromes. *Clinical Medicine*, 2, 501–4.

Simons, J., Franck, L. and Robertson, E. 2001. Parent involvement in children's pain care: views of parents and nurses. *Journal of Advanced Nursing*, 36, 591–9.

Singhal, A., Tien, Y.-Y. and Hsia, R. Y. 2016. Racial-ethnic disparities in opioid prescriptions at emergency department visits for conditions commonly associated with prescription drug abuse. *PLoS ONE*, 11, e0159224.

Smith, E. 2016. What a patient with learning disability would like you to know. *BMJ*. Available at BMJ 2016;355:i5296 (accessed 14 May 2017).

Sonntag, J. 2008. Doctors' involvement in torture. *Torture*, 18, 161–76.

Stacey, M. 1970. *Hospitals, Children and their Families: The Report of a Pilot Study*. London: Routledge and Kegan Paul.

Steppe, H. 1997. Nursing under national socialism. In Rafferty, A. M., Robinson, J. and Elkan, R. (eds) *Nursing History and the Politics of Welfare*. London: Routledge.

Stevens, B., Riahi, S., Cardosa, R., Ballantyne, M., Yamada, J., Beyene, J., Breau, L., Camfield, C., Finlay, G. A., Franck, L., Gibbins, S., Howlett, A., McGrath, P. J., McKeever, P., O'Brien K. and Ohlson, A. 2011. The influence of context on pain practices in the NICU: perceptions of health care professionals. *Qualitative Health Research*, 21, 757–70.

Stokowski, L. A. 2011. Managing relentless pain in cancer survivors. Available at www.medscape.com/viewarticle/737345_2 (accessed 26 May 2015).

Strong, P. M. 1979. Sociological imperialism and the profession of medicine: a critical examination of the thesis of medical imperialism. *Social Science and Medicine*, 13A, 199–215.

Svoboda, J. S. and van Howe, R. S. 2013. Out of step: fatal flaws in the latest AAP policy report on neonatal circumcision. *Journal of Medical Ethics*, 39, 434–41.

Tasca, C., Rapetti, M., Carta, M. G. and Fadda, B. 2012. Women and hysteria in the history of mental health. *Clinical Practice in Epidemiology and Mental Health*, 12, 110–19.

Taylor, B., Carswell, K. and Williams, A. C. 2013. The interaction of persistent pain and post-traumatic re-experiencing: a qualitative study in torture survivors. *Journal of Pain and Symptom Management*, 4, 546–55.

Tengvall, O., Wickman, M. and Wengström, Y. 2010. Memories of pain after burn injury: the patient's experience. *Journal of Burn Care and Research*, 31, 319–27.

Toye, F., Seers, K. and Barker, K. 2014. A meta-ethnography of patients' experiences of chronic pelvic pain: struggling to construct chronic pelvic pain as 'real'. *Journal of Advanced Nursing*, 70, 2713–27.

Trentman, T. L., Chang, Y. H. H., Chien, J. J., Rosenfeld, D. M., Gorlin, A. W., Seamans, D. P., Freeman, J. A. and Wilshusen, L. L. 2014. Attributes associated with patient perceived outcome in an academic chronic pain clinic. *Pain Practice*, 14, 217–22.

UNAIDS, UNDP, UNECA, UNESCO, UNFPA, UNHCHR, UNHCR, UNICEF, UNIFEM and WHO 2008. *Eliminating Female Genital Mutilation: An Interagency Statement*. Geneva: World Health Organization.

van Hecke, O., Torrance, N. and Smith, B. 2013. Chronic pain epidemiology and its clinical relevance. *British Journal of Anaesthesia*, 111, 13–18.

van Teijlingen E. 2015. Sociology of midwifery. In Deery R., Denny E. and Letherby, G. (eds) *Sociology for Midwives*. Cambridge: Polity.

van Wijngaarden, E., Leget, C. and Goossensen, A. 2015. Ready to give up on life: the lived experience of elderly people who feel life is completed and no longer worth living. *Social Science and Medicine*, 138, 257–64.

Visentin, M., Trentin, L., De Marco, R. and Zanolin, E. 2001. Knowledge and attitudes of Italian medical staff towards the approach and treatment of patients in pain. *Journal of Pain and Symptom Management*, 22, 925–30.

Vrancken, M. A. 1989. Schools of thought on pain. *Social Science and Medicine*, 29, 435–44.

Waitzkin, H. 1989. A critical theory of medical discourse: ideology, social control, and the processing of social context in medical encounters. *Journal of Health and Social Behaviour*, 30, 220–39.

Walker, J. 2012. *Researching Contested Illnesses: The Case of Chronic Fatigue Syndrome (CFS)*. Boston. Available at http://in-training.org/

researching-contested-illnesses-the-case-of-chronic-fatigue-synd
rome-cfs-90 (accessed 24 January 2016).

Watt-Watson, J., Stevens, B., Garfinkel, P., Streiner, D. and Gallop, R. 2001. Relationship between nurses' pain knowledge and pain management outcomes for their postoperative cardiac patients. *Journal of Advanced Nursing*, 36, 535–45.

Waxman, S. E., Tripp, D. A. and Flamenbaum, R. 2008. The mediating role of depression and negative partner responses in chronic low back pain and relationship satisfaction. *The Journal of Pain*, 9, 434–42.

Wenger, L. M. and Oliffe, J. L. 2014. Men managing cancer: a gender analysis. *Sociology of Health and Illness*, 36, 108–22.

Werner, A. and Malterud, K. 2003. It is hard work behaving as a credible patient: encounters between women with chronic pain and their doctors. *Social Science and Medicine*, 57, 1409–19.

West, C., Stewart, L., Foster, K. and Usher, K. 2012. The meaning of resilience to persons living with chronic pain: an interpretive qualitative inquiry. *Journal of Clinical Nursing*, 21, 1284–92.

Whiteford, L. M. and Gonzalez, L. 1995. Stigma: the hidden burden of infertility. *Social Science and Medicine*, 40, 27–36.

WHO, UNICEF and UNFPA 1997. *Female Genital Mutilation: A Joint WHO/UNICEF/UNFPA Statement*. Geneva: World Health Organization.

Wilkinson, I. 2005. *Suffering: A Sociological Introduction*. Cambridge: Polity.

Williams, A., Davies, H. and Chadury, Y. 2000. Simple pain rating scales hide complex idiosyncratic meanings. *Pain*, 85, 457–63.

Williams, A. C., Peria, C. R. and Rice, A. S. 2010. Persistent pain in survivors of torture: a cohort study. *Journal of Pain and Symptom Management*, 40, 215–22.

Williams, G. 1984. The genesis of chronic illness: narrative re-construction. *Sociology of Health and Illness*, 6, 175–200.

Williams, S. and Bendelow, G. A. 1998. In search of the 'missing body': pain, suffering and the (post)modern condition. In Scambler, G. and Higgs, P. (eds) *Modernity, Medicine and Health: Medical Sociology Towards 2000*. London: Routledge.

Williams, S. J. 2000. Chronic illness as biographical disruption or biographical disruption as chronic illness? Reflections on a core concept. *Sociology of Health and Illness*, 22, 40–67.

Williams, S. J. 2005. Parsons revisited: from the sick role to...? *Health: An Interdisciplinary Journal for Social Study of Health, Illness and Medicine*, 9, 123–44.

Wischmann, T. and Thorn, P. 2013. (Male) infertility: what does it mean to men? New evidence from quantitative and qualitative studies. *Reproductive BioMedicine Online*, 27, 236–43.

Wylie, C., Platt, S., Brownie, J. and Chandler, A. 2012. *Men, Suicide and Society*. London: Samaritans.

Yuxiang, L., Lingjun, Z., Lu, T., Mengjie, L., Xing, M., Fengping, S., Jing, C., Xianli, M. and Jijun, Z. 2012. Burn patients' experience of pain management: a qualitative study. *Burns*, 38, 180–6.

Zborowski, M. 1952. Cultural components in responses to pain. *Journal of Social Issues*, 8, 16–30.

Zimmerman, S. L. 2002. States' spending for public welfare and their suicide rates, 1960 to 1995: what is the problem? *Journal of Nervous and Mental Disease*, 190, 349–60.

Zisk, R. Y. 2003. Our youngest patients' pain: from disbelief to belief. *Pain Management Nursing*, 4, 40–51.

Zola, I. K. 1966. Culture and symptoms: an analysis of patients' presenting complaints. *American Sociological Review*, 31, 615–30.

# Index